BASAL READERS: A SECOND LOOK

Edited by:

Patrick Shannon
Kenneth Goodman

RICHARD C. OWEN PUBLISHERS, INC.
Katonah, New York

"Poetry can . . ." from *Pass the Poetry, Please!*
© 1972, 1987 by Lee Bennett Hopkins
reprinted by permission of Curtis Brown, Ltd.

© 1994 by Richard C. Owen Publishers, Inc.

Library of Congress Cataloging-in-Publication Data

Basal readers : a second look / edited by Patrick Shannon, Kenneth
  Goodman.
      p. cm.
    Includes bibliographical references (p.   ) and indexes.
    ISBN 1-878450-60-3 (pbk.) :
    1. Basal reading instruction.   2. Basal reading instruction—
Evaluation.   I. Shannon, Patrick, 1951— , II. Goodman, Kenneth
S.
LB1050.36.B38   1994
372.41—dc20   94-5745
                                                                  CIP

RICHARD C. OWEN PUBLISHERS, INC.
PO Box 585
Katonah, New York 10536

PRINTED IN THE UNITED STATES OF AMERICA

9 8 7 6 5 4 3 2 1

Contents

Contributors

Debbie Birdseye is a teacher in Corvallis, Oregon.

Patricia Crawford is a graduate student in Language and Literacy Education at Penn State University.

Carole Edelsky is a Professor of Education at Arizona State University.

Bobbi Fisher is a teacher in Sudbury, Massachusetts.

Mem Fox is a children's author and senior lecturer at Adelaide University, Australia.

Yvonne Freeman is a Professor of Education at Fresno Pacific University.

Kenneth Goodman is a Professor of Education at the University of Arizona.

Sandra Lawing is a teacher in Dare County, North Carolina.

Lisa Maras is a teacher in Buffalo, New York.

Kathy Mason is a multi-age primary teacher in Gilbert, Arizona.

Sharon Murphy is a Professor of Education at York University, Canada.

Bob Peterson is a teacher in Milwaukee, Wisconsin.

Elaine Schwartz is a graduate student in Language, Reading and Culture at the University of Arizona.

Patrick Shannon is a Professor of Education at Penn State University.

Timothy Shannon is on leave as Superintendent of Feather Falls School District, California and a graduate student in Curriculum and Supervision at Penn State University.

Preface

In 1986, Marc Gallant wrote and illustrated *More Fun with Dick and Jane* for the New Contemporary Reading Series. His intent was clear—he wished to poke fun at the old Scott, Foresman's primers while he satirized the 1980s in North America. In this new book, Dick, Jane, and Sally are grown, have children of their own, fly stunt kites, are divorced, use pooper scoopers for the new Spot, start cookie franchises, shop by phone, and "network." Their kids are devout consumers of popular culture with punk haircuts, Barbies and G.I. Joes, and Macs (but not Big Macs). For the forty-something crowd who were schooled with Dick and Jane (or their cousins in other basal series), Gallant's book is pretty funny.

Despite all these changes, Gallant's primer remains true to the original basal genre. *More Fun with Dick and Jane* starts with single words that label pictures of characters (*e.g.*, Dick), works toward sentences (*e.g.*, "Look, Look!" said Brad), builds "stories" out of these sentences (*e.g.*, A Walk with Spot), and ends with new vocabulary lists organized according to the page on which they are introduced. It is the replica of a student primer in every respect, and part of Gallant's humor comes from his juxtaposition of changing times in society with the traditions of schooling.

In a much less clever fashion, this is what Bonnie Freeman, Ken Goodman, Sharon Murphy, and I tried to accomplish when we wrote the *Report Card on Basal Readers* for the National Council of Teachers of English. We gathered information that demonstrated that the ideas that underlie basals and the articulation of those ideas into the anthologies, workbooks, tests, and other paraphernalia were behind the times in terms of language theory and research, child and adolescent development, and teachers' education. We substantiated our concerns with references to particular basal materials, research on basal production and use, and policies within publishing and schooling that seek to control teachers and students during reading lessons. We acknowledged trends in basals and reading programs that we thought were more contemporary, and we closed with 28 recommendations for teachers, administrators, teacher educators, professional associations, researchers, basal authors, editors, and publishers, and policy makers. We thought we were clear, fair, and comprehensive; and we stand by the *Report Card on Basal Readers* as the best analysis of basals and their use.

Our commentary caused a different reaction than did Gallant's. While many seemed willing to laugh at the dated content of basals and were certain that all had changed in the genre of primers that Gallant so successfully lampooned, they were not willing to accept the *Report Card*'s naming of problems with the very idea of basals—that teachers and students must be controlled during lessons in order to teach and learn reading. Perhaps, this was to be expected given the economic interests that surround this more than $400,000,000 per year industry. Rather than address the issue of control, however, basal publishers and authors did what they do best. They attempted to camouflage this control in newer, brighter, bigger, and better materials and sell them under the banner of the latest rhetorical slogans popular among literacy educators regardless of the compatibility of the ideas that underlie basals and the ideas that underlie the rhetoric. In fact, some publishers' representatives attempt to sell their materials by claiming that basals have met the recommendations at the end of the *Report Card on Basal Readers*.

Of course, they have not met those recommendations, and for this reason we have assembled a group of educators to analyze the latest basal editions. We chose not to write this second report alone because we think it important that these concerns are not tied singly to our work and that other voices—children's authors, teachers, and administrators as well as other teacher educators—are heard on these issues. This second look does not duplicate our first look. We have not reiterated the *Report Card*'s analyses of the history, economics, production, or language of basals in this new volume, all of which is still relevant to understanding even the most recent basal productions. The new analyses add considerable depth and breadth to our original concerns and add new topics (*e.g.*, Spanish language, writing instruction, and multiculturalism) as well as new voices.

We do not intend to write or edit a third look at basals in the future. With this volume and the *Report Card on Basal Readers,* we hope that we are sufficiently clear and convincing in our efforts to explain how the ideas of control that underlie basals must change if basal materials are to become contemporary in both content and form. However, we shall fight all urges to produce *Report Card III* or *The Revenge of the Report Card on Basal Readers*, even if basal publishers, editors, and authors cannot change their minds.

Patrick Shannon

Foreword

LOTS OF CHANGES
BUT LITTLE GAINED

BASALS IN READING INSTRUCTION: IS THERE CHANGE AND IS IT REAL?

How much have basals changed and how much has reading instruction changed since our first *Report Card on Basal Readers*? My best answer is Tevye's favorite answer in *Fiddler on the Roof*: ''I don't know!'' Change, particularly in the real life of children, is hard to measure. And over the decades, change in basals has been more superficial than real.

Some actual data on change in basal use and practice come from a surprising source: the 1992 Report of the National Assessment of Educational Progress (NAEP) Reading Report Card[1] (Executive Summary).

---

[1] The National Assessment of Educational Progress is funded by the federal government and prepared and administered by Educational Testing Service in Princeton, New Jersey, under contract with the National Center for Educational Statistics of the U.S. Department of Education.

If we examine these data while examining the basal texts themselves it will help to give us a more complete picture of how basals and their use are changing.

Whereas we quoted research in our first report that showed 90 percent to 95 percent of American elementary classrooms using basal readers to some extent, NAEP now reports a marked shift in at least fourth-grade instruction.

> More than one-third of the fourth graders (36%) had teachers indicating they relied solely on basal materials for their reading instruction, although about half (49%) were being taught through a combination of both basal and trade books. Only 15% were being taught without basal materials.[2]

There's considerable regional variation: 14% of Northeast teachers say they primarily use tradebooks. Only 7% of Southeast teachers report the same, while basal use is reported by 45% of Southeast teachers, and only 28% of those teachers in the Northeast and West.

The report shows a contrast between what teachers *say they do* and what children say they are *required to do*. Only one-third of the teachers said they use worksheets and workbooks daily. But half the children say they use them daily. Even that is encouraging—first because *only half* are suffering from workbook/worksheet abuse, and second because it shows an awareness of teachers that they should be doing things differently than they are. All the basals we examined still include workbooks and various forms of worksheets as components. These data appear to show a marked decline in their use by teachers.

---

[2] Just to show the problem with statistics, this figure is reported as 12 percent and 13 percent in two other places in the report. It's possible that the percentages reflect different base totals for the particular tables, but that's not made clear in the report.

Both children and teachers agree that half of all fourth-grade pupils *read silently* and *read books of their own choice almost every day.* Books of their own choice! Wow! No prior study on a national scale has shown this involvement of children in choosing what they are reading in school. Furthermore, the more often children read books of their own choice, the higher their mean scores on tests. This remarkable finding reflects what teachers reported about the "instructional approaches" their pupils were experiencing:

> Eighty-two percent were receiving at least moderate emphasis in whole language instruction. 88% were receiving moderate emphasis in literature-based reading, and almost all (98%) were receiving moderate emphasis in integrating reading and writing skills.

While 61% said they gave "moderate emphasis" to phonics, only 11% were getting "heavy emphasis."

Also encouraging is the report that those in literature-based and whole language programs scored significantly higher than average, while those in heavy phonics programs scored well below those receiving little or no phonics. Those children with teachers reporting primary emphasis on tradebooks scored better than those in classrooms primarily using basals. Those using both scored in between the two nationally.

Of course, this is *fourth-grade data.* Yet there is logic in assuming the figures would be at least as good for primary classrooms, because there is every indication that whole language and literature-based programs have the most solid support among primary teachers. Evidence from the report shows that, by fourth grade, *44% of the children say they "read for fun" almost every day* whereas only 13% say they almost never do so. That seems to reflect habits of reading and a view of reading and themselves as readers built up over the primary years.

Ten states are not reported in the national assessment. This reflects their concern over the NAEP's release of state-by-state comparisons. Their concern is quite justified: the *Los Angeles Times,* in reporting the low overall position of California in the assessment, ranking only above Mississippi, the District of Columbia, and Guam, blamed the stress on literature-based reading and neglect of phonics. Ironically, these last three show the highest rate of heavy emphasis on phonics in the country: 40 percent in DC, 29 percent in Guam, and 22 percent in Mississippi. What complicates these state-by-state comparisons is the relatively high percentage of minority students in some states as compared to others. Our schools are less successful in educating non-mainstream children, and our tests aren't very successful with them either.

While it is commendable that the NAEP looked at the use of instructional materials and instructional emphases and even attempted to compare students who had these different experiences, these categories show considerable confusion on both their part and on the part of teachers. Particularly as they get into specifics, the framers of the NAEP seem to have a hard time identifying and defining significant instructional innovations. For example, they focus on the use of workbooks and worksheets, but muddy the waters by suggesting the nature of these may be changing in basals. Our look at new basals suggest that the terminology is changing more than the fundamental nature of these materials. One aspect NAEP didn't look at is a trend in school systems such as Tucson Unified School District to adopt a "literature-based" basal, but not the workbooks and worksheets. That must be a significant trend because basals show some attempt to separate out references to the workbooks. For instance, Harcourt Brace Jovanovich (1993) offers a separate Teacher's Edition for their workbook.

NAEP highlights the fact that a high percentage of teachers report that they have children write about something they've read. Lisa Maras, in her study of writing in the basals (Chapter 5) found that basal writing exercises are often loosely based on reading selections. Such writing was usually highly constrained and often went off on a tangent from the reading.

NAEP asked children if they discuss what they read with friends and family and found that most do. That's not surprising, but it's good to know. It surely shows that children think that what they are reading is worth talking about. But NAEP didn't ask about discussion opportunities in the widespread use of literature sets and literature study groups within classrooms. It is quite likely that children learn to enjoy talking about what they are reading in school and carry that over outside of school.

Clearly there is a shift not only in how much reliance there is on exclusive use of basals. As I'll show, there is also some continuing change in the basals themselves. And there seems little doubt that it's possible, in classrooms using basals, for pupils to be having considerable opportunity to read silently from books of their own choice. It's possible for teachers to be using basals, either exclusively or in combination with tradebooks, and also believe that they are emphasizing literature and/or whole language. Virtually all teachers believe they are integrating reading and writing. Some of this reflects the language in the teacher's manual that teachers using them accept. But part of it is likely to be due to real change in the basals and real changes in how teachers do or don't use them.

SOME CHANGES IN NEWER BASALS

More Literature and Less Editing

The publishers have clearly responded to the demand that reading instruction include more literature. They're editing less of the original written text, although the use of excerpts is dominant.

Heavy Use of Picture Books in Early Grades

The print text is now usually intact, but the picture text is drastically reduced and homogenized. And pseudo-picture books that have the look of a picture book, but the controlled vocabulary of the older basal primer stories, are in some basals. Big books are now almost universal in basals.

Abundant Use of the Terminology of Whole Language

Process writing, strategic reading, language integration, literature study, and other popular terms appear in the teacher's manual. Sometimes these terms are carried over into the program, as when the trivia questions and follow-up activities are relabeled "response to literature" or when activities are called "meta-cognition." Harcourt Brace Jovanovich uses "running record" as a term for almost any informal assessment:

"We believe," says Silver Burdett-Ginn (1991), "that reading is a conversation between a reader and an author. . . . We believe that the teaching of reading begins with the child—the child's language, the child's own experiences, the child's world."

Here's Harcourt Brace Jovanovich (1993):

> We believe that young children bring to the classroom some knowledge of literacy, upon which teachers can build a love of reading and writing. . . . We believe that through a more holistic approach to teaching reading and language arts, students will discover the connection between reading, writing, listening and speaking. . . . We recognize that each classroom is a unique learning environment and that effectively managing the resources within that environment is a challenge. We are committed to helping teachers meet the needs of all students in a literature-based classroom.

Inclusion of Tradebook Collections in the Basal Packages

This inclusion is sometimes, but not always, as common reading materials for the class as groups. In some cases this leads to the puzzling practice of the whole class reading the same book at the same time. Some basals provide basalization in the form of exercises and workbook activities to go along with the tradebook reading.

Inclusion of Writing Activities in Lesson Sequences

This often includes but goes somewhat beyond the fill-in-the-blanks and half-sentence answers of the older workbooks, but it is always controlled and structured and rarely leaves the student any real choice or control over the writing process.

Some Apparent Effort to Deal with a Changing Market by Appearing to Provide Alternate Ways for the Programs to be Used by Teachers with Different Pedagogic Beliefs and with Different Populations of Students

Harcourt Brace Jovanovich labels some manual pages "Teacher's Choice," suggesting the teacher may choose or not choose to use them. Of course this implies the teacher must use the pages that aren't marked this way. Sections on inflections (adding -s to nouns and verbs), vowel (letter-sound relationships), final consonants (letter-sound relationships), and classifying (classify "objects" into groups) are not labeled Teacher's Choice, but Integrated Curriculum (science, art, math, music, social studies) is. So are Integrated Language Arts and Building Independence through Reading.

Some Continuing Attempt to Appear More "Multicultural" in Content and Representation of Ethnic and Handicapped Groups and in Gender Balance

Although all programs have improved their records on inclusion, they more often than not treat multiculturalism as if it were a separate issue from literature study.

THE NEW BASALS: SPOTTED LEOPARDS AND CATCH-22'S

Can the basal leopard change its spots? Is there a Catch-22, an intrinsic contradiction, in the nature of basals that ultimately makes them stay the same in spite of any apparent changes? The evidence from our second look at basals strongly supports the conclusion that, in spite of these changes, a basal is a basal is a basal, still a spotted leopard, still caught on its own internal inconsistencies. That's because the publishers have not changed the fundamental justification of the basal, their claim that it is a complete, inclusive, sequential, and scientifically designed program, which, if followed closely, will teach children to read. They still sell their products to school administrators with the promise that the materials themselves will make up for differences in teacher competence or learner difference. And there are still plenty of administrators who mandate that teachers must closely follow the manuals and produce results on the end-of-unit skill tests.

Listen to Silver Burdett-Ginn:

> It's an extraordinary time to be teaching reading. There's fresh understanding of the complexity and wonder of the reading process. There's real excitement about great children's literature and the catalytic power to develop language abilities. Wherever you

turn, an educator is talking about *literature-based reading, integrated language arts,* and *holistic approaches to
language.* These alluring phrases seem so full of promise for kids and teachers. The question is: *How can you
turn these into responsible, manageable classroom applica-
tions?* (emphasis mine)
You need a framework. . . . *World of Reading* provides
this framework . . .

This program, like Harcourt Brace Jovanovich's,
says it offers teachers choices. Yet the implication is
clear that teachers need the basal to structure and control their work. No matter what they promise and
no matter their intent, basals are caught in their own
promise that a program must be structured, sequenced, and controlled, with a didactic framework
to control teaching and learning.

American basals have another given: they are intended to reach the full national market. Publishers'
and their parent companies' huge investments in
them are based on that. That makes their promise to
be inclusive of everything necessary for all children
to be able to learn to read (and now also to write)
even more of a problem for the publishers. Their response is eclectic inclusivity. Here is the full range
of components in Harcourt Brace Jovanovich's 1993
copyrighted offering as the publisher organizes them:

Kindergarten: *The Treasure Tree* (itself an inclusive
package)
Core Kit: Big Books; Theme Books; Read-Aloud
Anthology, Literature Posters, Music Cassette, Pic-
ture/Word Cards/Teacher's Editions and The Treas-
ure Tree Assessment. Also offered: Treasures to
Share: An HBJ Library; Little Books, and Big Book
Cassettes

Literature Components
Students' Anthologies (1–8)
Big Books (1–3)

Big Book Cassettes
Literature Cassettes (1–8)
Treasures to Share: An HBJ Library (1–8)
More Treasures to Share: Literature Perspectives
(4–8)

Teacher Materials
Teacher's Editions (1–8)
Picture Cards (1)
Letter and Word Cards (1)
Phonics Connections Kit: Literature Treasures (1)
Instructional Charts (1–3) and Transparencies
(1–8)
Harcourt Brace Jovanovich Staff Development
Series

Student Support
Writer's Journal (1–8)
Practice Book (1–8)
Integrated Spelling (1–8)
Project Cards (1–8)

Family Activities
Take-home Books (1)
Family Involvement Activities (1–6)

Assessment Choices
Unit Skills Assessment and Teacher's Edition
(1–8)
Unit Holistic Assessment and Teacher's Edition
(1–8)
Unit Integrated Performance Assessment and
Teacher's Edition
Portfolio Assessment Teacher's Guide (K-8)
Individual Inventory for Reading and Writing
(1–8)
Group Placement Tests, Teacher's Edition with
Copying Masters (1–8)
Computer Management System (1–8) (Apple and
IBM)

Learning Technology
Laserdisc (1–8)
Reading Software (3–8) (Apple)

Second-Language Support
    Second-Language Support Manual (1–8)
    Transition for ESL Students (1–6)
    ESL (1–5) (Posters and Manual for skill development)

Basal publishers have always had the temptation to include many components and to integrate their texts for reading, spelling, writing, handwriting, and English. They give purchasers the impression that they must buy everything or the program "won't work." They seem to feel now that they must be inclusive to meet their promise of integration and being holistic, and they must offer choices, such as in their assessment practices, to meet the changing views of assessment among potential purchasers. That opens the lid of Pandora's box, however. Teachers and administrators are seeing the possibility of buying only some components and not others. Whether cause, effect, or both, they also seem to be opting in greater numbers to not buy the basals at all. In spite of the publishers' claims that structured basals are essential to reading development, the NAEP data seem to show a strong tendency to treat them, where they are used, as materials to use with trade books as part of an instructional program. Only about a third of classrooms in the study were reported by teachers as using basals exclusively.

The different assessment alternatives show the publishers' awareness of the changes going on in the field. There is demand for more authentic and process-oriented assessment. But they can't make a decision to move to exclusive holistic assessment or portfolio assessment. So they continue to offer everything. One alternative that is missing, of course, is the on-going, in-process assessment that teachers do without any tests or published materials.

Another real development is that the school and trade divisions of the publishers have had to combine their efforts to produce a basal package of tradebooks.[3] Historically, these divisions have had little to do with each other, and have often been cool or hostile in their relationships. The history leaves some problems: if a trade title is included in a program component, either the trade division has to agree to keep it in print for the duration of the basal program (indefinite) or allow the basal division to use the plate to reprint as needed. Using tradebooks published by other companies is even more complex. On the other hand, the huge school market for tradebooks is really being opened and exploited as never before. At least part of the huge increase in sales of tradebooks, over 500 percent in ten years, must be due to greater school purchases.

The inclusiveness is also eclectic. It leads to this kind of statement:

> Reading is an active, ever-evolving process, from a child's first halting attempts at decoding to the wondrous ability to construct meaning (Harcourt Brace Jovanovich, 1993).

Most people who believe that reading is meaning construction do not believe that reading development starts with "halting attempts at decoding" which can be separated from the "ability to construct meaning." The programs, however, provide components and lesson sequences which separate "decoding" (a euphemism for sounding out) from meaning construction. And they do not facilitate teachers sorting out these inconsistencies—though an increasing number seem to be able to do so. Some teachers have even

---

[3] The term tradebook refers to books published for sale to the trade, that is through bookstores. It has come to be a term to refer to children's literature as contrasted with textbooks such as basals. Publishers who produce both have always had totally separate school and trade departments.

suspected publishers of using "doublespeak." That is language particularly chosen to confuse and obfuscate.

Sadly, there will be schools and classrooms where they will try to use all the components, all seven assessments, all the teacher choices on the still common belief that everything is in the program where it is for some scientific reason and that leaving even one question or practice page out may lead to deficiencies in the pupils later in life.

THE FUTURE OF BASAL READERS

There is every reason to believe that the trends shown by the NAEP survey will continue. Teachers are moving away from basal dominance and slavish adherence to the imperatives of the teacher's manual. Publishers have shown that they recognize this in their use of the holistic terminology and the inclusions of more literature in the anthologies and tradebook packages among their program components. At the same time, the publishers have been unable or unwilling to change in a more fundamental way. They still have as their central premise that their didactic framework is a necessary part of reading and writing instruction. That makes every experience a child has in the program a controlled and instructional one. Publishers may feel that by keeping this central premise that they have co-opted the movement toward whole language and literature-based literacy pedagogy. And some will surely intensify their efforts to follow an eclectic "everything for everybody" approach in developing their programs.

I asked one publisher's representative about the differences in the 1993 edition of his company's basal. He said, "We had a 1989 and a 1991 edition and now the 1993 edition. The 1991 edition did great but the 1993 edition isn't doing very well." "Any idea why?"

I asked. "We made too many concessions to the whole language folks. They're not buying basals," he replied. I suspect he's at least partly right. If publishers change their products they may lose old customers without gaining new ones. But then maybe they would lose customers without changing too.

I'm encouraged by the continuing growth of the number of informed and empowered teachers who have realized that they don't need basals to build the reading and writing of their pupils. In a fairly short period of time there has been a shift in teachers of perhaps ten percent away from any basal use altogether and a much larger shift away from total reliance on basals. If in the next few years this momentum continues, then publishers will be forced to make further changes.

One possible change would be to make the tradebooks the central component of the programs, either dropping the anthologies altogether or making them single volume anthologies of the original texts, much as *Bill Martin's Sounds of Language* incorporated the *Little Owl Series* originally done for Holt, Rinehart and Winston. Even if publishers do that, it doesn't mean they would give up on basalization. Some smaller publishers and some school systems are imposing three-part lesson plans and skill and vocabulary drills on trade books.

Another possibility would be to give up on single programs for the entire national school market and to begin producing targeted programs aimed at different segments of the market. That's not new. Publishers have offered targeted programs for sale to groups wanting more and less phonics, for parochial schools, for regions, for slower learners, for Spanish speakers, and so on. Their survival may depend on moving away from trying to convince everybody their main program is just right for them and moving toward offering programs designed explicitly for identifiable groups. A problem with this is the states and large school systems that still make single adoptions, but that's changing, too.

Ironically, a major restraint on the basal publishers' ability to respond to the new realities of American classrooms is their size and clumsy decision-making structure. In *Report Card on Basal Readers* we had to keep revising the section on how many publishers controlled the major share of the basal market because of mergers happening within publishing houses as we wrote. That trend hasn't stopped. School publishing is now controlled by mega-corporations with decision-making far removed from the people who know the field best and who are best able to respond to trends. I'm told that the editorial staff loses sleep worrying about whether they'll be working the next morning and for whom.

The upside to this situation is that some large niches have emerged, to be filled by smaller, newer publishers. I suspect that this may be the direction from which the most innovative responses to the new demands of empowered teachers will come. These new houses involve and consult teachers in these innovative efforts.

I want to close on a realistic note. There is change in the experiences children are having in reading instruction and in the materials their teachers are using. But the changes are not simple and directions of future change are by no means clear. The changes that have occurred in basal reading programs are primarily responses to changes in classrooms and not causes of those changes. We said in the original *Report Card on Basal Readers* that the only sure way that teachers could bring about changes in basals is to stop buying the current offerings. Some teachers have done that. The extent to which teachers continue to move away from basals will determine the extent to which the basals continue to change.

Kenneth Goodman

1

"I DON'T THINK THESE COMPANIES HAVE MUCH RESPECT FOR TEACHERS:" LOOKING AT TEACHER'S MANUALS

PATRICIA CRAWFORD AND PATRICK SHANNON

A representative from a major publishing company made the following statement, "We've changed. These are completely different books."

After Kenneth Goodman's and Yetta Goodman's address at the 25th annual conference of the Keystone State Reading Association, a representative from a major publishing company made the following statement, "We've changed. These are completely different books. That's why we could kill Goodman for criticizing us and distorting things the way that he has." (Keystone State Reading Association, 1992). The salesman's response was a reasonable one. Basal publishers view their new programs as not only being dynamic, exciting, and meaningful, but also as being fundamentally different from past publications. They have responded to the call for quality literature by including popular stories by well-known authors. They have met the criteria for authenticity by maintaining the original story language and some original artwork. They have met the demand for connecting learning experiences by organizing these stories by themes. And they have provided much-in-demand whole language resources such as author information, predictable stories, and big books. What else is a company to do? In the mind of this basal representative, Goodman and his whole language friends have become nothing short of nags. Whole language advocates have asked for change, gotten it, and are still not happy. What do they want?

We take this representative at his word and acknowledge that publishers have made a number of positive changes in the 1993 editions. However, it is necessary to take a closer look to determine the nature of these changes and to see if basal programs have changed in the fundamental ways necessary to be considered "completely different books." If basals have truly changed, what is it that continues to drive the wedge between the positions of basal publishers and people such as Goodman and his associates?

The history of basal readers is a relatively short one. Although basals have their roots in the series of reading books that were developed during the eighteenth century, it was not until this century that commercial reading materials began to take the shape and form that we know today (Venezky, 1987). Basal reading series, with their grade-specific texts and accompanying components, have come to characterize reading instruction in the United States (Shannon, 1987, 1989, 1990). When adults are asked to recall their most vivid memories of learning to read in school, they often respond by naming such things as reading groups, ability levels, workbooks, and thick, hardbound anthologies of stories. Although these elements may be among the most memorable aspects of basal reader instruction for students, none of these features can be considered the driving force behind the program. Rather, it is the teacher's manual that has driven basal programs.

In a discussion about reading instruction, a prospective teacher noted the following:

> I remember seeing teachers with these big teacher books and I always wanted to be a teacher because it just seemed mysterious. Little things teachers did . . . they had the teacher's manual and grade books and the chalk and the red pens. It's part of the image of being a teacher. It kind of becomes ingrained in you.

The goal became to not only provide guidance, but also to virtually teacher-proof the curriculum.

TEACHER'S MANUALS

The idea of a teacher's manual has indeed become ingrained within our educational system. These guides became commonplace in the 1920s and have been expanding with each succeeding edition since that time. Based on behaviorism and Thorndike's laws of learning, these guides typified the United States' deep belief in the power of science (Shannon, 1987, 1989). The early manuals contained directions for the teacher and were designed to promote systematic instruction. As the manuals expanded, the goal became to not only provide guidance, but also to virtually teacher-proof the curriculum so that all students would be guaranteed a successful reading education regardless of the ability, or lack of ability, of their teachers. This was accomplished through the double-edged sword of content and language found in the teacher's manuals. The content of the manual ensured that the method of choice for the teaching of reading in the United States would be direct systematic instruction. The nature of the directive language of the annotations established the publishers' voice of authority. While the introduction of the teacher's manual may have made teaching easier for the inexperienced teacher, it also shifted the elements of power, choice, autonomy, and control out of the hands of individual teachers and into the hands of textbook publishers, where they have remained for seventy years (Apple, 1986; Shannon, 1987, 1989). Venezky (1987), a basal author himself, notes that:

> One of the great ironies in the development of the modern basal is that as teachers received more and more preservice and in-service training in teaching reading, the authors of reading texts assumed that teachers knew less and less and expanded the teacher's manual and textbook instructions accordingly (p.252).

As the teacher's manual expanded and became increasingly directive in nature, it no longer reflected the school curriculum, but instead it became the curriculum. In his description of *The American Schoolbook,* Black (1967) states:

> The textbook and its even heftier manual also will determine how almost any given subject will be taught . . . . Moreover, the teacher's manual organizes the course for the teacher, describes most of the teaching techniques she will use, and provides hundreds of student homework assignments, discussion and test questions, as well as the answers (p.3–4).

It is the teacher's manual, with its scope and sequence charts, directive annotations, and programmed lessons, that has traditionally determined the direction of instruction (Austin & Morrison, 1963; Barton & Wilder, 1964; Chall, 1967, 1983; Durkin, 1981). Therefore, this is the arena in which fundamental change must take place. Although publishers have made many changes in their 1993 editions, these series can only be considered fundamentally different if there has been change in both the content and the directive, driving nature of the manual itself.

OUR ANALYSIS

In order to see if these changes have taken place, we analyzed the 1993 teacher's manuals from three major publishing companies: Houghton Mifflin, Macmillan/McGraw-Hill, and Scott, Foresman. In order to look at material at both the primary and intermediate levels, we focused on the first- and fifth-grade manuals for each series. We looked at these documents in terms of form, content, philosophy, and language. We believed that if real change had taken place, we would see changes in the following areas: First, the scope and sequence, with its hierarchy of isolated skills, would be diminished. Contextuality would be emphasized and the teacher's manual would no longer determine when and how skills would be taught to generic groups of students. Second, the teacher's manual would be much less directive in nature. Publishers would no longer tell teachers how to teach by dictating methodology or by providing the type of scripted material that is better suited for technicians than for professionals (Shannon, 1987). Third, the content of the basal program itself would change. For both teachers and students, choice would be a hallmark of the program. There would be many opportunities for children to transact with quality literature and to engage in meaningful reading and writing in a variety of ways. If these changes had taken place in the 1993 editions, we would find ourselves having to agree with the basal representative and would be able to conclude with him that the new basals were fundamentally different from past editions.

The 1993 manuals are durable, attractive, spiral-bound books. Each of the manuals contains introductory statements that articulate the philosophy of the series. These statements show that publishers are well aware of the changing face of literacy education. Although the format may vary, current literacy issues such as shared reading, integrated language arts,

Publishers would no longer tell teachers how to teach.

Basal publishers rely heavily on outside experts to plan instruction, add credibility, and provide both direct and indirect guidance to teachers.

reading-writing workshops, and multicultural issues are all addressed in either the preface or appendix of each manual.

Experts

Each of the manuals reviewed features a number of well-known literacy experts on their boards of authors and consultants. Women and minorities are represented. Children's literature experts such as Violet Harris and Joan Glazer (Houghton Mifflin, 1993) are represented, as are emergent literacy theorists such as Elizabeth Sulzby and Leslie Mandel Morrow (Scott, Foresman, 1993). Even William Teale, editor of *Language Arts*, a journal of the National Council of Teachers of English, is present on these boards (Houghton Mifflin, 1993; Macmillan/McGraw Hill, 1993). Macmillan/McGraw Hill (1993) weaves their program philosophy throughout a section that features short biographical pieces on the series' well-known authors. They make the following statement in this section:

> Individually, these fifteen authors represent some of the most highly acclaimed reading/language arts educators in America. Collectively, they are a synergistic resource that far exceeds the sum of its parts. They're competent, and committed to taking philosophy into practice (Macmillan/McGraw-Hill, p.vi).

Scott, Foresman's manuals not only have a distinguished board of authors, but also go a step farther and put teachers in direct contact with a "board of experts." Scott, Foresman consumers are given a toll-free number to use for further guidance in implementing their series. Teachers are encouraged to call the toll-free professional hotline and "Let our team of experts fill you with confidence and fresh ideas" (Scott, Foresman, 1993). So, it seems that basal publishers rely heavily on outside experts to plan instruction, add credibility, and provide both direct and indirect guidance to teachers, by way of the teacher's manual.

Although the term may be dead, the spirit of scope and sequence is alive and well in the new basals.

Scope and Sequence

The term scope and sequence has all but disappeared in the 1993 basals. Publishers now speak in terms of "program framework" (Houghton Mifflin, 1993), "overview of reading strategies" (Scott, Foresman, 1993), and "goals and outcomes" (Macmillan/ McGraw-Hill, 1993). Although the term may be dead, the spirit of scope and sequence is alive and well in the new basals as given evidence by the following:

> The goals and outcomes of Macmillan/McGraw-Hill Reading/Language Arts are organized into five categories or domains. The domains represent the major areas of literature-based integrated language arts instruction and assessment. Within each domain, there are subcategories of specific strategies and skills (Macmillan/McGraw-Hill, 1993, level 5, p.T45).

This statement is followed by a 38-page scope and sequence chart that lists 163 separate skills to be covered throughout the elementary program. Although Scott, Foresman (1993) devotes only five pages to scope and sequence, they list 190 major skills and strategies (p.12). Houghton Mifflin (1993) devotes only two pages to their "program framework." However, they list 126 different skill areas and then refer teachers to a separate publication, the *Program Framework Scope and Sequence Booklet* "[f]or a more detailed level by level breakdown" (p.126). As in basals of the past, these manuals define their scope through a long series of subskills that are organized according to broad domains or strands (Goodman, *et al.*, 1988). The subskills in these frameworks are given form in the manual's lesson plans. Each one of these series has scope and sequence charts that dictate that teachers address isolated skill areas such as capitalization, initial and final consonants, short and long vowels, main idea, sequencing, fact and opinion, and so on (Houghton Mifflin, 1993; Macmillan/McGraw-Hill, 1993; Scott, Foresman, 1993). And, while lessons sometimes give students opportunities to use skills in the context of meaningful reading and writing, more often they promote the use of skills that are either completely isolated or ones that can only be considered to be contextualized by the letter of the law. For example, Scott, Foresman uses a poem entitled "The *Pancake Man*" (emphasis ours) as the basis for a "decoding workshop." Children are encouraged to respond to this poem by working through several activities designed to build *-an* word families (Scott, Foresman, 1993, Level 1A, pp.A.19e–A.19f).

In reviewing the 1993 teacher's manuals, we noted two distinct language registers used within these publications. The first, found predominantly in the introduction and philosophy statements of each edition, is a register that is appropriate for use among professional colleagues. It is a language of choice and empowerment. For example, the following statement is made in the Macmillan/McGraw-Hill manual: "Together we'll address the educational and philosophical issues that researchers and educators nationwide have identified as key . . ." The language reflects a comradery between publishers and teachers. However, both the language and the comradery vanish as the introduction ends and the lessons begin.

The language register within the pages of the lessons themselves is authoritarian and reflective of a situation in which directives are given and clearly expected to be carried out, as in the following examples:

Tell children that they will be reading a story that counts different animals. Help children remember the words to the song "Old MacDonald Had a Farm." Can they revise it slightly to turn it into a counting song like this (Scott, Foresman, Grade 1, p.A.38e)?

Discuss relating words by synonyms and antonyms. Display these adjectives. . . . Point out that the paired words are synonyms, words that mean the same or nearly the same thing (Macmillan/McGraw-Hill, Grade 5, p.163).

Discuss the illustration on page 71. Ask: What kind of store is this. (a grocery store) How can you tell? (by the things on the shelves and the things the big sisters ask for) (Houghton Mifflin, Grade 1, p.71).

Although the language seems to imply a sense of choice, the sheer repetition of this "suggestion" in each lesson seems to be directive in nature.

The use of the imperative form is rampant within the lesson plans, with publishers often telling teachers not only what to do, but also what to say. The manuals speak with the voice of authority to an audience that does not seem to have a voice at all. In some cases, the tone has been softened through the use of hedge words such as "may" or "might." For example, Macmillan/McGraw-Hill includes a "Vocabulary Focus" section with each lesson. It is usually introduced with a statement similar to, "You may want to use the following activity before or after reading." (Macmillan/McGraw-Hill, Grade 5, p.121). Although the language seems to imply a sense of choice, the sheer repetition of this "suggestion" in each lesson seems to be directive in nature.

After reviewing the 1993 teacher's manuals, we found little cause for celebrating. Although the quality of the anthology has improved, little else is different. The new manuals still follow scope and sequences of skills, albeit under an assumed name—"framework," "overview," or "goals." They still embed stories in skill lesson frameworks with often heavy-handed directives for teachers and students. Despite the representations and the rhetoric of the experts in the statements at the front of the manuals, little has changed—other than packing more into each lesson, from the basals of the 1970s and 1980s. If the experts are really in charge as the philosophy statements claim, we wonder why the heart of basals, the teacher's manuals, has so little correspondence with the research and writing of the experts outside of their responsibilities as basal authors. The 1993 basals are not completely different as the Keystone salesman suggests; they do not even seem to be representative of the fine work of the experts the publishers employ.

SILENCED VOICES

We asked three practicing teachers who currently use basals in their classrooms, three practicing teachers who do not use basals, and three prospective teachers who were in the final stages of their course work, but who had not yet done their student teaching, to look at and comment on the 1993 teacher's manuals we had examined. During individual interviews, each participant examined two teacher's manuals, each one from a different basal series. Participants reviewed the introductory philosophy statements for each manual and then stated their expectations for a program that espoused such beliefs. Participants then looked at sample lessons within the same books and made judgments regarding whether or not the individual lessons were compatible with the beliefs described within their opening statements. Finally, participants were asked to describe their ideal plan for the reading-writing classroom and to tell whether or not they would choose to use a basal system such as the ones they had analyzed, if given the option.

The participants in our study found much to agree with after reviewing the statements of philosophy for each series. Teachers made many positive comments

regarding the companies' stated commitments to literature-based instruction, multiculturalism, reading for
meaning, and emergent literacy theory. After viewing
a fifth-grade Houghton Mifflin manual, one teacher
commented, "This sounds very good. They want children to become life-long readers as all teachers do. I
agree with what this says."

Based on the language of the introductions, study
participants had high expectations for each series.
Teachers stated that they would expect to see the following things in reading programs that made such
claims:

*Based on the
language of the
introductions,
study participants
had high
expectations for
each series.*

- early book experience
- strong links between
  reading and writing
- strong home-school
  connections
- few worksheets/little
  seatwork
- many opportunities
  for discussion
- skills addressed in
  context
- more freedom

- interesting stories
- natural language
- reading and writing
  workshops
- hands-on activities
- less emphasis on skills
- cooperative learning
- emphasis on choice

Although participants seemed to view the statements positively and held high expectations for the
series, they also tended to view them with guarded
optimism and a bit of skepticism. After reviewing one
philosophy statement a teacher remarked, "This
looks very commercial. It makes me wonder about
the series." Another noted, "This looks nice, but I'm
suspicious." These teachers seemed to wonder if the
content of the basals would deliver on the promises
made in the introductory materials. One prospective
teacher cut to the heart of the matter by observing,
"I like this, but the real issue is what's in the rest of
the book. I want to see the rest of it before I make a

Participants did not seem convinced that the structure of lessons had changed significantly.

decision." The real issues do not lie in what publishers say, but rather in what publishers do. And what publishers do is more closely related to the content, form, and language of their actual lessons than it is to their philosophy statements.

Lesson Format

Respondents were less enthusiastic about the format of the lessons and the suggested activities than they were about the publishers' stated philosophies. After reviewing the lessons, participants did not seem convinced that the structure of lessons had changed significantly enough to fit with the rhetoric of the philosophy statements (Willinsky, 1990). One teacher stated that "[The manual] gives the teacher several choices about how to read the selection." But, then she also noted, "This much is still the same as always—predict, read, respond." Another teacher asserted that "Although they've made changes in the literature, the basals are still very much the same as far as format." A prospective teacher expressed disappointment regarding the lesson format by noting, "The lessons are too structured. This isn't what I expected . . . There are nice stories in here, but it pretty much seems like the regular basals from before."

All nine participants were also displeased with the treatment of stories. One prospective teacher stated, "There's too much here. It seems like they beat the story to death. I think kids would get bored and want to move on even if it was a good story." Another commented, "There's too much here. There are so many questions to ask. The children wouldn't enjoy the story. Breaking the story up like this would really make it dull."

Teachers also felt that the manuals included too much unnecessary skill work with each lesson, noting that many of the skills were taught in isolation and that there was too much seat work. A teacher commented. "Here they have you introducing terms that don't necessarily need to be introduced. Maybe the kids already know these words. Then, it's a waste of time. They want them to fill in the blanks. There's not a lot of context."

Participants also expressed dissatisfaction with the terminology used within the skill development sections of the annotations. Terms such as "journal" and "workshop" created different expectations among teachers than what was actually delivered in the lessons. On the issue of journals, one prospective teacher asserted, "This isn't really a journal. It's just one more marketing technique. The whole thing seems organized to death. It's too slick."

Along the same lines, teachers questioned the idea of basal-directed workshops. One teacher asked, "Why do they call this a workshop? These are more activities to go with the story—extension activities. It's more of the same. It's sure not the kind of workshop where kids have choices." Another asserted, "Now a language workshop! This doesn't seem like a workshop either. This is really English and spelling. Why don't they just say that? Things haven't changed." Finally, one teacher criticized the use of the term workshop and accused the basal publishers of using such terminology in an effort to gain sales:

> They have enough different types of workshops here! I find this all very amusing. They're covering every base. They do it so that more people buy it. It's all sales . . . the publishers jump on the literature bandwagon. They'll kill it. They think that more is better.

Language within Lessons

In reviewing the teacher's editions, the study participants noted the use of language within the annota-

Participants also expressed dissatisfaction with the terminology used.

tions and directions provided for the teachers. One person stated, "This is very much directed. You don't have much choice. This tells you exactly what to say." Although all participants agreed that each of the teacher's manuals reviewed were directive in nature, it was noted that word choice made a difference in the ways that the directions were perceived. Lesson plans that invoked the imperative were looked on less favorably than plans that offered suggestions and choices. One teacher noted, "It's very directive, but the language seems gentler. It doesn't seem like they are telling you what to do or are talking down to you. They use a lot of words like 'might' and 'may.' I feel like I'd have more of a choice." Another stated, "They say that you 'might comment'. They don't just tell you 'comment about'. It's how they say it. That makes a big difference."

This issue of language is the one area of discussion on which prospective and practicing teachers seemed to agree initially, but then later parted company. Although members of both groups noted and criticized the specificity of the annotations and the directive nature of the language, practicing teachers stated consistently that they did not want or need such guidance, whereas prospective teachers wavered in their position. Also, practicing teachers expressed a sense of "numbness" to the presence of such directions and the use of the imperative, while prospective teachers expressed a sense of indignation at being addressed in such a way.

Prospective teachers seemed to be surprised by the specificity of the directions that accompanied the selections. One woman seemed puzzled after looking at a lesson and said:

> "I would probably do this anyway without anyone telling me . . . I don't take the language personally, but we did go to school for four years. I'm intelligent enough to decide what I want to do. I don't take it

personally, but I wouldn't follow it either. It seems like there's just a lot of extraneous information here."

Publishers seem ready to exploit the fears of new teachers.

Another prospective teacher commented, "This makes us seem like we're stupid. If something's important to the story, it's going to come out. I'm going to say it. They don't need to tell me what to say."

Despite the assertions that they did not want or need these types of guidelines, these prospective teachers seemed to waver at certain points. Each of them expressed a concern about their upcoming first year of teaching. One woman who initially looked at the annotations stated simply, "I don't need this." However, she later pondered, "I don't know if I'd do what they say to do. Maybe as a first-year teacher when I don't know as much . . . but, as I become more experienced, I don't think I'd need to look at this." Another prospective teacher did a complete turnaround. After describing her desire to develop a whole language curriculum, she then reviewed a teacher's manual and stated, "The directions don't offend me. I want it there where I can get at it when I need it. It's all laid out."

It seems that the prospective teachers who participated in this study were torn between their personal beliefs about teacher choice, professional decision-making, and literacy education on one hand, and their fears about their upcoming experiences as first-year teachers on the other. In short, they are still defining their spots within the field of education and testing the theoretical and practical limits of their philosophies of education. Publishers seem ready to exploit the fears of new teachers by creating a sense of dependence on their expertise by way of directive teaching manuals and gimmicks such as Scott, Foresman's "professional hotline." A practicing teacher noted the seductiveness of the new basals for teachers who are in this position. She noted:

The new basals might help some people who are in a state of transition. But, I'm afraid that they wouldn't want to move away once they got comfortable with this format. After a few years of using these, they would become just like the old basals. Teachers would rely on them in the same way. You wouldn't have to be thoughtful. You wouldn't have to plan. Just open it up and do what it says.

The practicing teachers in our study took a different position than the prospective teachers when analyzing the language of teacher's manuals. These participants stated that they tended to ignore most of the guidelines provided for each story, and emphasized the fact that they did not rely on the annotations. One person noted, "They tell you what to say, but they call them think alouds. That's the new thing. I wouldn't use these at all because I never have the book in front of me when I teach . . . I never read from the text." Another person asserted, "They tell you what to say here. I might say it, I might not. But, I'd say it because it made sense, not because it was written here."

In commenting on the annotations, one teacher linked the type of language included in them with the underlying nature of basals:

I've really never met anyone who follows all of this stuff. Most people don't even read it. I mean, how could you? There's so much here that you'd never have time. You'd be there forever, just trying to read through it. There's too much . . . I know what I'm doing, so I just ignore it. But I think that just having this here might perpetuate the prescribed nature of basals.

None of the practicing teachers we interviewed indicated that they would choose to use such a series. Rather, they expressed a desire to use "real books," in a school setting that provided resources, support, and a sense of autonomy and control. One teacher stated:

> I'd rather just have books over an anthology any day. I want to get real books into their hands—let them touch them, hold them. That's what they need. I wouldn't mind having some support or resources for certain books, but you can get those without having a whole basal series.

This teacher has been able to do what the basal publishers have not. She has re-envisioned the school literacy program as one in which teachers are given ample support and resources in a form that does not strip them of their voice or power. A number of teachers in this study expressed concern for the needs of both new teachers who were just beginning their careers and older teachers who had been teaching traditional reading lessons for a long time. They recounted their own personal journeys with and away from basals and acknowledged the difficulties that can be encountered when teachers are left to build their own whole language curriculum without the support of colleagues and administrators. Teachers want and need support for genuine change and lasting professional development. However, this can not come from the pages of a teacher's manual.

NOT COMPLETELY DIFFERENT

Despite "quality" children's literature, fewer altered stories, and some progressive philosophical statements, the 1993 basal teacher's manuals remain very much the same as their predecessors. They are still based on the assumption that learning to read requires a standard, tight, and lengthy scope and sequence of skills and the control of teachers' teaching and students' reading. That is, the manuals not only provide a general framework for learning, they im-

Economic concerns are at the heart of the changes in the 1993 basals.

pose step-by-step directives toward reading, and often put words in the mouths of teachers and students. If the teacher's manuals have not changed, then the basal series cannot change. The contradictions between publishers' rhetoric and deeds were not lost on the teachers we interviewed. "I'm not sure I like this. They can't seem to let go of the old."

Other teachers we interviewed were able to theorize why these contradictions remain within basals. "I don't think these companies have much respect for teachers. They're only making the changes so that they can make money." "The basal profits come from selling. They'll do anything to make it seem like their program can fit with what you're doing. That's why they try to position themselves as being both conservative and progressive at the same time." According to these teachers (and we agree) economic concerns are at the heart of the changes in the 1993 basals. Depending on where you look in basals you can find information to support a variety of theoretical positions on reading and teaching. But when you look at what counts—the assumptions on which the program is based, which are encoded in the teacher's manuals, you can see that the homicidal intent of the Pennsylvania basal salesman is not because Goodman and other critics have it wrong. On the contrary, it is because these critics name this contradiction and explain that nothing really has changed, that there is a rhetorical bounty on their heads. But, it is not just Goodman and noted critics who must be eliminated in order to keep basal sales high, because teachers are ready to act:

> These [philosophy statements] look like advertisements. It's too slick. It doesn't look scholarly. All of this introductory information reminds me of a salesman—and I'm ready to kick him out the door.

2

EXERCISE ISN'T ALWAYS HEALTHY

CAROLE EDELSKY

It was easier to spot the exercises in the older basals; the books and workbooks were obviously full of them.

When he talked about twitches versus winks, Clifford Geertz (1973) gave convincing justification for the need to consider people's purposes. The surface behavior is the same, but there are major underlying differences in meaning, interpretation, and intention. So it is with the differences between the reading and writing instigated by basal readers—even the newest ones—and the reading and writing people undertake, for the most part, outside of school. What students do in response to basals are reading or writing exercises; but exercises in reading or writing are not what they do outside of school.[1]

It was easier to spot the exercises in the older basals;

---

[1] The distinction between a reading exercise and a nonexercise is one of a set of theoretical distinctions that need to be considered in planning for optimum literacy education

the books and workbooks were obviously full of them. Sometimes, pages were labeled as such (comprehension exercises, vocabulary exercises, and so on). More often, it was the form itself that signaled "instructional exercise"—blanks to fill in, boxes to connect, segments to underline or circle. The 1993 basals rarely use the term "exercise" as part of the title for a page.

---

for all children. (See Edelsky, 1991, Chapter 5 for a complete discussion of these distinctions.) The set takes (print) literacy as the superordinate category. Literacy includes every use of print as print (but not as material for wrapping fish or decorating a room [*e.g.,* a string of V's as a border on a wall]).

The first distinction under the broad category of literacy is reading versus NOT-reading. That is, some uses of print as print (literacy) do not result in the creation of a text meaning for the user. Making or looking at the V's on the above mentioned wall would be an example. Another would be naming the letters on a chart during an eye examination. These are cases of literacy, but not reading. The difference here is whether someone is creating a text meaning for herself.

The next distinction is exercise versus nonexercise. When people read—and also when they are engaged with print but they are NOT-reading (creating no text meaning)—they are either doing exercises or not. An example of reading as an exercise is reading a short story and possible answers as part of a reading test. An example of NOT-reading as an exercise is reading nonsense syllables in a reading workbook. An example of reading as a nonexercise is reading a letter from a friend. An example of NOT-reading as a *non*exercise is naming letters on an eye chart when having one's vision checked.

Yet another distinction is subject/object: whether the print user has a lot of control or a little in her print use. The social relations among all those connected with that instance of reading usually determine whether someone is using print as a subject or not. In addition, the print itself may position a reader as an object. For example, vanity license plates offer "tricks with print" that exert excessive control over the reading process itself (*e.g.,* forcing the reader to suspend confirmation until she "gets the trick" and depriving the reader of the use of all cueing systems).

And by and large, they do not ask students to connect boxes or circle chunks of print. Nevertheless, they are as packed with exercises as their predecessors were—more sophisticated exercises, exercise wolves wearing "literature-based" and "process writing" sheepskins—but exercises just the same.

What is wrong with that? If we want children to learn to read and write, why not have them do reading and writing exercises? (I will use the single term "reading" to stand for both reading and writing, except where I mean writing only.) After all, presumably, reading exercises transfer to "regular" reading, just as scores on reading exercises presumably predict how well someone reads "regularly." The problem is that the presumption of transfer and its partner, prediction, are just that, presumptions. There is no evidence to support them. It is just as likely—and more theoretically defensible—that children learn to do reading exercises during reading time in school and that they learn to read for pleasure, information, and so on when they are actually reading for pleasure, information, and so on both in and out of school.

What there *is* evidence for, evidence that comes from a voluminous body of research that claims to be about reading but that is almost entirely about reading exercises, is that learning to do reading exercises "transfers" to other exercises and that being able to do reading exercises predicts being able to do other reading exercises. Most researchers, most educators, and most of the lay public do not consistently distinguish between reading a book "for real" and reading it as an exercise. People may feel the difference, but they don't usually incorporate that feeling into their research designs or into their desires for particular kinds of reading instruction.

A few literacy researchers (Torbe, 1988) have begun to differentiate contrived school reading from other reading, to separate writing in school from writing out of school (Black & Martin, 1982; Moss & Stansell,

A few literacy researchers (Torbe, 1988) have begun to differentiate contrived school reading from other reading.

1983; Wilde, 1988), to sort out school-sanctioned from unsanctioned writing (Florio & Clark, 1982). Some (Erickson, 1984) analyze the social relations that differentiate the two; some look at the different texts produced (Edelsky & Smith, 1984); and some contrast the underlying processes (Harste, *et al.*, 1982; Edelsky & Draper, 1989). This research gets theoretical support from Soviet activity theory (Leont'ev, 1978), which suggests that any change in goals or motives constitutes a change in the activity itself.

While a few literacy researchers account for something like an exercise/*non*exercise distinction, most researchers (as well as most educators, students, parents, legislators, and so on) fail to make that distinction. That failure is crucial. It lets educators fill the school day with exercises in the belief that learning to do reading exercises for school is the same as learning to read for life. It lets the public take scores on exercises (in the form of criterion and norm referenced tests) as proof of how well their schools or their children are doing. And it permits reading instruction to become completely dependent on a basal technology, which in turn, is totally dependent on reading exercises.

Reading to find information needed for living is a different activity—a different social practice, a different discourse practice, a different literacy task—from reading to find information needed for proving that one can read. It is possible to do one well and not the other (Altwerger & Resta, 1986). As long as reading instruction focuses on exercises (whether commercially-prepared basal exercises or homemade exercises), it is depriving students of opportunities to learn to read "for real" (as a nonexercise).

My argument about an exercise/nonexercise distinction and my complaints, therefore, about even the newer basals derive from an understanding of the nature of language and language learning. The basic theoretical premise is this: *written language is language.*

If written language is language, then it has the characteristics of language. Thus, like oral language, written language is a system of abstract conventions for making meanings in a context (Halliday, 1985). Like oral language, the "default" function of written language is informational (Gee, 1989). Written language, like oral language, is shared socially and organized socially. Both oral and written language are always tied to contexts because language is always used in a particular place at a particular time among particular people for particular purposes (Hymes, 1970). Like oral language, written language is reflexive; *i.e.*, it is created through contexts and, at the same time, it helps create the context in which it is used. Both oral and written language are ambiguous. They always require interpretation; they can always be used for multiple purposes; and they can always convey multiple meanings. Each is also predictable, offering cues for meaning, and redundant, offering more than one set of cues.

Language is not primarily learned through exercises.

Moreover, if written language is language, then it is learned like language. And language is primarily learned through actual use with others who really use the language with and in front of the learner. Language is not primarily learned through exercises. Though language is learned *through using* it, in general it is not deliberately *used for* the purpose of getting and giving language lessons. Purpose, in other words, is all-important. Using language, as opposed to doing language exercises, means using conventions in sound or print or signed gestures to make meaning for some *communicative* purposes (*e.g.*, for warning, informing, soothing, arguing, inviting, teasing, complimenting, gossiping, plotting, entertaining, inquiring, persuading, apologizing, and so on). *Using language primarily for being instructed in language itself or for being evaluated on language itself is an exercise.*

Purpose is the distinguishing feature between exercises and nonexercises. Purposes for using language within an event are intimately tied to the meaning of that event (*i.e.,* what is that event *about?*). People do not usually interact with each other for the primary purpose of evaluating (or being evaluated on) language use.[2] When that *is* the purpose, the event is *about* evaluation, and the language use (written or oral, lengthy or brief, dull or "creative") by the one being evaluated constitutes an exercise. Conversely, when everybody knows the event is about evaluation, language is used within it, not for some communicative purpose, but for demonstrating proficiency. People also do not generally enter into interaction with each other for the purpose of instructing or getting instructed in language use.[3] Again, when this *is* the overall purpose, then the event is *about* instruction. Even if the reading or writing lesson *looks* like, for example, letter writing, what the students write is merely an exercise in letter writing.

Can school events ever be about anything except instruction or evaluation? Can students' purposes for using written language inside the "official" curricu-

---

[2] It is no contradiction to note that as hearers, during nonexercise language use for communicative purposes, we always evaluate those we hear, and that as speakers, we talk in ways that will let us be evaluated in certain ways. That is, it is true that we can't give messages without also giving *off* messages (Goffman, 1959). When we appraise people's language use during daily life (when the stranger gives us directions or a friend tells us about a book she has read or when we read a letter-to-the-editor that contradicts our own opinion), it is primarily the *person* we are appraising—her ideas, her status, her origins. We are not evaluating her talk simply for the sake of evaluating language use.

[3] When adults direct babies to "say 'mama,'" they *are* entering into interaction for the purpose of instructing. Young children's repeated requests for labels ("wha' da?"), however, may be talk to get attention or to be playful rather than talk to get a lesson on talk. In the case of both adult and child, however, such talk for the purpose of giving (getting?) language lessons represents only a small fraction of daily adult-child exchanges at home.

lum ever be communicative? Must students' purposes be primarily for taking part in reading instruction (and thus being a good or at least an obedient student) or for proving proficiency as a reader? That is, does the institution of schooling necessarily turn any officially sanctioned student reading into an exercise?

Bloome & Bailey (1990) would say yes. They maintain that all activity in school comes into being for the purpose of instruction and therefore nothing can be "authentic," not even a vocational education project like building a house which someone will live in. I disagree. Some classroom projects have the potential to override their instructional purposes. If projects are big enough and if students have taken them on as their own, the multiple tasks required by those projects are no longer exercises. Learning has become subordinated to production, as Minick (1985) has characterized apprenticeships. For example, if children put out a monthly community newspaper with an out-of-school circulation and if that newspaper matters to them for some reason other than getting a grade, many of the embedded tasks (like writing headlines, preparing a table of contents, turning notes into a readable account, and so on) are then done for the sake of the newspaper. Instruction on headline writing, in that case, is not instruction for the sake of instruction but instruction for the sake of the newspaper.

Instruction on and evaluation of language is not ruled out, then, in classrooms where children read as a nonexercise. What is eliminated is instruction/evaluation of reading for the purpose of instruction/evaluation of reading. When the curriculum is made up of nonexercises—when both teachers and children read to escape into a story world, write to think their way clear on things that are really on their minds, read to find out more about something they are intensely interested in, write to get what they want, read to be entertained, write to help themselves remember what

If projects are big enough and if students have taken them on as their own, the multiple tasks required by those projects are no longer exercises.

they want to remember—teachers do give lessons on reading and writing and they assess children's reading and writing. But those lessons and assessments are done to facilitate the nonlanguage-learning purpose (entering into a story world, thinking more clearly, finding out, and so on). As with a twitch versus a wink, there is a world of difference between getting a lesson on using context clues because the story lends itself to instruction on using context clues versus getting that lesson because the story was so compelling that the child wants to tape it for younger children and needs to read it with more precision. The latter reason is an instance of the theoretical principle that people learn language through using it for something other than language learning.

Basing reading instruction on such a theoretical principle requires very different classroom conditions than are presumed by the current exercise-dependent basal technology. A nonexercise basis for reading instruction requires that learners have significant choice over what they read, that activities are frequently child-initiated, and that all children do not have to do the same thing. It implies a great likelihood that many projects and topics will arise spontaneously, that projects will be fine-tuned to the locality, that projects will be undertaken for some purpose other than instruction or evaluation of reading and that other purpose is the child's real purpose; it is not just the ostensible purpose behind that lurks the teacher's instructional purpose, that many projects will connect to the community and have an impact beyond the classroom walls.

In nonexercise reading, other people play very different roles than the teacher does in reading exercises. When someone writes an apology, recipients accept or refuse; they don't evaluate the spelling. When a neighbor recommends a book and maybe reads us a passage, we may read the book ourselves; we don't seize that opportunity to teach "reading with expression" or to "check comprehension." That is, the others in the literacy event, along with the reader or writer, use the print communicatively. Moreover, in nonexercises, others sometimes act as coliterates, which allows the original print user to remain active in a chain of literacy events. The apologizer may restate the apology; the friend asks us how we like the recommended novel and we recommend one in turn. *The major difference, however, between reading exercises and nonexercise reading is the reader's purpose. If someone is reading for the sake of taking part in instruction in reading or for the sake of being evaluated in reading, it is an exercise.*

The others in the literacy event, along with the reader or writer, use the print communicatively.

EXERCISES IN THE NEW BASALS

The authors of at least three major 1993 basals (Houghton Mifflin, Macmillan/McGraw-Hill, Scott, Foresman) have tried to take account of recent instructional and theoretical issues. The texts are full of children's literature. The teacher's manuals use trendy terms; they talk about theme work and cooperative learning; they ask questions about story elements and genres; they assign shared reading and interactive reading; they refer to personal response, strategies, and invitations, performance assessment and portfolios, the writers' craft, predicting and confirming, emergent reading, and concepts of print; they give teachers suggestions for working with children whose native language is not English and with children with "special needs" or who are "at risk." Clearly, the basal authors were trying to make basal reading instruction congruent with a variety of theoretical understandings (*e.g.*, reading as an act of interpretation and meaning construction, reading and writing as interdependent), responsive to a diverse population, and centered on "authentic" literacy activities.

Basal-generated authentic reading, however, is an oxymoronic phrase. Basals must be infused with pretense, just as they must be filled with exercises. A basal technology begins with certain views: there are reading skills (rather than skilled readers); skills can be separated from their contexts of use; skills can be learned and taught for their own sake without regard for communicative purposes. Basal activities, therefore, are by necessity exercises.

The exercise problem is twofold: first, the activities that go along with a story unavoidably turn into language exercises (sometimes oral, sometimes written); and second, since the stories become excuses for assigning numerous exercises, reading the story also becomes an exercise. *To repeat, reading exercises take place in events that are primarily about instruction in reading for instruction's sake or evaluation of reading for evaluation's sake, events when readers are reading mostly for the purpose of going along with reading instruction (which includes both getting reading lessons and demonstrating reading proficiency).*

If basals must be loaded with exercises and pretense, the new basals indeed meet that requirement. They get children to write phony letters, take part in phony debates, sit in phony literature circles, keep phony journals, and carry out phony projects. In connection with Taro Gomi's "Coco Can't Wait," Macmillan/McGraw-Hill's *A New View, A to EZ Handbook* (Grade 1, Level 3 teacher's manual) tells teachers to "invite" children to write letters to Coco *as though* they were Grandma or write to Grandma *as though* they were Coco. As one of their choices, they may write *as though* they are in the midst of trying to meet the other character (the characters repeatedly miss each other as they urgently try to connect). The child who accepts this "invitation" knows the letter has no live intended addressee and will not be mailed. Moreover, the child knows that given the intense efforts both

Grandma and Coco are making to find the other, neither would interrupt their quest to write a letter.

Scott, Foresman's *Teacher's Guide to Celebrate Reading*
(Grade 3) politely assigns topics for students' journals
and even assigns the type of structural unit the child
is to create—paragraphs, lists (students "might write
paragraphs about the origins of their names in journals" [p.C.6e]; "students can write a list of names
they would like to have been named and explain
why" [C.7]). Thus, what should be a vehicle for relating to another person (an interactive or dialogue journal) or for personal exploration (the personal journal)
becomes an informal essay or short quiz. The "journal" in Houghton Mifflin's *Fast as the Wind* (Level 5,
volume 1) isn't even an essay test: it asks for responses
to questions and provides blanks to fill in and directions for what to respond to. Houghton Mifflin also
has children writing a warning sign about the dangers
of a lagoon (p.15C) even though there is no actual
lagoon and no one who needs to be warned.

Scott, Foresman suggests that teachers "stage" a
debate (*Bridge to Celebrate Reading*, p.6), and staged it
is! Teachers are advised to make a chart listing the
points to be made by each side in the debate. After
the chart is made and the points made known to all,
the teams are assigned. The reason for debating—to
figure out and deliver clinching arguments—is eliminated. All that remains for the teams to do is to mouth
the words of the premade chart. Houghton Mifflin
(p.29A) suggests a "literature discussion circle" in
which children are supposed to discuss "a selection"
in small groups, even though if their teacher has followed the Teacher's Book, the children have already
spent days talking about this selection page by page.

Pretense isn't the only problem. The new basals
also mislead teachers. Macmillan/McGraw-Hill (*A to
EZ Handbook*, p.209), for instance, informs teachers
that "the cumulative structure" of *Hattie and the Fox*
"is designed to help children practice chunking" and

It is hard to imagine that Mem Fox's cumulative structures were really designed to teach chunking.

implies (p.212) that a key value of *Coco Can't Wait* is that the text gives students "an opportunity to practice and experience words such as *lives, of, hill, mountain, wanted, here, wait, minute,* and *hello.*" It is hard to imagine that Mem Fox's cumulative structures were really designed to teach chunking rather than to give verbal pleasure or that a value worth noting in Taro Gomi's text is an opportunity to practice words. Nevertheless, such suggestions, coming as they do from the authoritative teacher's manual, are likely to be taken seriously by teachers and conveyed to children.

The reason for putting children up to pretense and also for misleading teachers is that basal authors have not solved the purpose problem. Even though they frequently refer to setting purposes for reading, they end up trivializing the idea. "Purpose," in basal readers, means either the teacher's instructional purpose (*e.g.,* "read to identify main ideas") or a focusing purpose ("have children predict what Coco is having trouble waiting for") to help children answer the questions the teacher will ask when he or she next interrupts the reading. "Purpose" in a basal technology does not account for the *child's* purpose(s) for reading or writing that particular text, nor does it include an understanding of the notion of communicative purpose.

Basal authors seem to have made an effort to make the activities "purposeful," though. That is why they suggest letters, debates, literature circles, journals, skits, and research projects. But committed as they must be to instructing and evaluating particular skills for their own sake and for using particular stories to teach or evaluate particular skills, they can't carry it off. The letters, journals, debates, and so on can't help but turn into exercises.

That happens in part because of the phony set-ups (write a letter that will go to no one, have a literary discussion about a story that has already been talked to death, write a research report although no one will use the information, do a project on some topic [fashionably termed a "theme"] that has already been planned in detail by someone else). A suggested skit does not have young children play-acting a story for the purpose of entertaining themselves and others. Instead, the teacher's guide (Macmillan/McGraw-Hill, p.211) suggests that teachers assign a topic, get children to perform the skit on demand, fill in a workbook page on putting on the play, and labels the page a "performance assessment opportunity" for the teacher. Children are sensitive to the overall meanings of events; and one key way classroom events get their meanings is from what teachers are really interested in. When the teacher is advised (Macmillan/McGraw-Hill, p.220) to use children's play-acting to check their inclusion of major events in the story and their understanding of characters' roles, he or she will give children clues about the real meaning of the event: not entertainment (by composing a well-wrought improvisation) but evaluation.

If teachers and students treat activities as exercises because of phony set-ups for specific activities, they also turn specific activities into exercises because each activity is affected by the total context in which it occurs. That context—the total basal package—includes obvious exercises for all children (whether they need them or not) on consonant blends and short vowels, and workbook pages that focus on vocabulary exercises (trendily labeled "strategies") and proofreading sentences for spelling and punctuation. Running through the package is a view of comprehension that is generally word-focused rather than interpretation-focused. For example, Scott, Foresman's *Comprehension Workshop* (p.C23a) is subtitled "Figuring Out New Words." The total basal package also includes so many activities per story (*e.g.*, 32 *pages* of them for the 20-*sentence* story "Coco Can't Wait") that it practically screams the message: the stories don't count. In the

The package offers far-fetched gimmicks to liven up the more exercisey exercises.

total package are multiple means of controlling readers' responses too closely (*e.g.*, through multiple questions on every page).

The package offers far-fetched gimmicks to liven up the more exercisey exercises. For instance, Macmillan/McGraw-Hill's teacher's guide (p.229) suggests drawing a soup pot so children can "drop words that rhyme with *pot* "into the soup." Apparently, the authors believe the visual image will evoke the meaning and one possible lexical label that would then trigger a list of rhyming words. But the picture could also signal "pan," "tureen," "pressure cooker," or "crock." Moreover, some child could just as well see the soup pot and think "soup," generating a rhyming list like "croup," "loop," etc. Regardless, it is doubtful that a picture of a soup pot will help a child who is having trouble rhyming.

The total basal package also directs teachers to parcel out stories in paragraphs, to interrupt the oral reading of a text (by teacher or by student) with frequent questions, to point out "facts" about words, to spoil the suspense in a story by interrupting it precisely at the points of tension (as Houghton Mifflin directs teachers to do with a pedantic guided tour about "rising actions" and "falling actions" (pp.22, 28).

Not only are many activities patent fakes (*e.g.*, the phony letters), not only does the total package steer teachers to use the stores and activities as reading instruction for instruction's sake and reading evaluation for evaluation's sake, but the worst consequence is that all of this makes it almost impossible for a child to treat these activities as anything other than exercises. Why would a child follow someone else's directions and write a warning sign to an imaginary traveler about a nonexistent lagoon while being sure to use particular words from a story? Certainly not to really warn anyone. The only likely purposes a child can have for such writing have something to do with taking part in instruction or evaluation for their own sake. And how could a child read for the purpose of giving herself up to a story world when she is directed to read a twelve-page story (Houghton-Mifflin, pp.17–28) that is interrupted by 26 lessons on "reading new words," "figurative languages," "noting details," "identifying rising action," "vocabulary development," "sequence of events," "idiom," "creating the setting," "making inferences," "identifying climax," "critical reading/thinking," and "identifying falling action?" She can't help but read that story for the purpose of taking part in reading instruction for instruction's sake; *i.e.,* as an exercise in story reading.

If people spend significantly more time reading as an exercise, they will surely be inexperienced at reading for real.

The new basals, like the old ones, continue to take time away from reading "for real." Instead, they fill the reading/language arts time with exercises. In other words, they teach "reading instruction"—this decade's version of it to be sure, a version that exploits literature and that appropriates the surface form of genres like journals and letters, but leaves out what those genres are for—but "reading instruction" nonetheless. They don't teach reading for the world, reading for communicative purposes, reading for real, reading as a *non*exercise.

If people spend significantly more time reading as an exercise, they will surely be inexperienced at reading for real. What is not sure is a question of value. What kind of reading do we want? It is not at all certain that we can have both. The discourse practices that people acquire are the ones they participate in (Gee, 1991). As Leont'ev explained, when purposes change, the activity changes. Reading a bus schedule to demonstrate chart-reading skills is a different activity, a different discourse practice, than reading the bus schedule in order to arrive at work on time. If we want people to be able to read as an exercise, the new basals are fine. If, however, we want people to be able to *use* written language in their lives, they have to have lots of experience *using* written language in their lives. That means schools will have to give up their addiction to basal technology.

3

LOOK! LOOK! WHO STOLE THE PICTURES FROM THE PICTURE BOOK?*

KENNETH GOODMAN, LISA MARAS, AND DEBBIE BIRDSEYE

There is good and bad news in the newer versions of basal readers. Some of the good news is that newer basal readers are including more literature in their current versions. The bad news is that the literature is being basalized. Part of the good news is that a lot of picture books are being used in the early levels of basals. The bad news is that to fit them into the format and structure of the basals, they're being changed from picture books to illustrated stories, and that makes them less authentic, harder to read, and less enjoyable. Ironically, by fitting them into the didactic framework of the basals, picture books are made harder for children to predict, to make sense of, and to learn from. In this chapter we won't cite every ex-

* A longer version of this chapter appears in *The New Advocate*, Winter, 1994.

Illustrations and written language are different semiotic systems, or ways of symbolically representing meaning.

ample from every basal, but the examples we will discuss are typical of the use of picture books in all the basals.

THE PICTURE BOOK GENRE

Picture books are sometimes called twice-told tales, but that is not true in the sense that pictures and print each supply a complete telling of a story. Illustrations and written language are different semiotic systems, or ways of symbolically representing meaning. They work together in such a way that the whole is more than the sum of what each contributes to the telling Together, illustrations and text create a unified text, resulting in the creation of complex images and meaning that cannot be created by the parts alone (Schwarcz and Schwarcz, 1991).

In picture books we get the advantages of both semiotic systems. Written language progresses in a largely linear fashion: words, lines, and pages come before or after each other. This sequence is essential to comprehension. Pictures, on the other hand, use two-dimensional surfaces to present a unified whole with all of the aspects and details accessible to our eyes simultaneously (Schwarcz and Schwarcz, 1991). There is no prescribed direction for viewing or making sense of the pictures, though in the whole text the order of the pictures and their position with regard to the written text is important.

Illustrations do more than provide pictures to go along with the text. They can be descriptive, repeating what the written text says, they can be narrative, interpreting the print, or they can be both. "In fact, without the pictures, we might not understand the meaning of the words" (Shulevitz, 1985). The pictures often provide details such as setting, metaphors, and ideas not offered in the text (Schwarcz and Schwarcz, 1981). Characters can be created pictorially in ways the words can never do. Reading the words without seeing the pictures would be like listening to television with a blank screen.

ILLUSTRATIONS AS A NON-ALPHABETIC WRITING SYSTEM

Only when the written text and the illustrations are read together can the story be fully appreciated and comprehended.

Picture books are both a literary genre and an art form. The illustrations, while providing an aesthetic experience, also have the power to convey meaning and tell stories. The pictures constitute a non-alphabetic writing system such as those that predate alphabetic writing. Because the pictures represent subtleties so well, the print text can be kept simple. Authors can use unfamiliar words, confident that the pictures will provide a context to make the words and their meanings predictable (Ardizzone, 1980). Illustrators also recognize that pictures are themselves a writing system. While "pictures extend, clarify, complement, or take the place of words" (Shulevitz, 1985), it is equally true that "an illustration can tell a story without the help of the text. . . . [it] is a form of independent writing. It is pictorial literature" (Duvoisin, 1980).

READING PICTURE BOOKS

Margaret Meek says that "a page in a picture book is an icon to be contemplated, narrated, explicated by the viewer. It holds the story . . ." (1988). The meanings of the story are translated into the semiotics of the visual. "Gradually the reader learns that the narration is made up of words and pictures, together" (Meek, 1988). Only when the written text and the illustrations are read together can the story be fully appreciated and comprehended.

Illustrations are read much like the print in the text. The reader brings his or her own experiences to the

Because of the two semiotic systems inherent in the picture book genre, changing either system changes the whole.

text and illustrations, and from this transaction constructs meaning. The picture book, however, is much richer in cues for the reader than a usual print text, and the developing reader uses the pictorial cues to create a rich context for the print cues. At the same time the information from the print confirms the comprehension of the picture sequence.

Picture books can be enjoyed and understood by readers long before they can make sense of the print. That makes it possible for them to experience rich narratives not limited to simple vocabulary. Once children have had a picture book read to them, they do not have to be able to read the words in order to read the book. In fact, as they turn the pages and view the pictures they are able to supply much of the written text they have heard. The non-alphabetic telling of the story frames the written language and is important to the literacy development of young readers (Meek, 1988). The illustrations provide support for young readers as they make sense of the print. "The pictures are at once exciting and reassuring, all in the cause of helping the child appreciate [the] story" (Roberts, 1981, p.5).

Readers use the same strategies to read illustrations that they use to read text. They gather, evaluate, and use information through sampling, predicting, inferring, confirming, and self-correcting (Goodman, *et al.*, 1987). Readers of illustrations have "to learn which of the pictorial events carries the line of the story . . ." (Meek, 1988, p.13). To do this readers use sampling strategies, selecting the cues from the illustrations that are most useful to understanding the story. Readers make predictions and inferences from illustrations to help with their understanding of the story (Kiefer, 1983) based on what they sampled. The illustrations also help readers to confirm or reject their predictions and inferences. Readers can self-correct and monitor their reading of the text by matching their reading with the illustrations. Because of the two semiotic systems inherent in the picture book genre, changing either system changes the whole and also changes the relative ease with which they can be read.

PICTURE BOOKS: MAKING THEM FIT INTO BASAL PROGRAMS

In looking at how trade books are treated in basals, we found a strong pattern. The words are not being edited, but the pictures are. Basal editors are taking liberties with the illustrations from the literature they have chosen for their programs, having them cropped, reduced, and rearranged. They often undergo subtle color changes, and worst of all, they are frequently deleted. This is not a haphazard process. The loss of carefully crafted illustrative sequences is the result of fitting picture books into the constraints of instructional materials. In examining the transformation of picture books into basals we looked at several features.

Choice of Illustrators and Illustrations

When an author is not also an artist, a publisher must put a great deal of thought and effort into choosing the right illustrator for a manuscript. Illustrators must concern themselves with the significance of the story; the pictures should integrate with and complete the story (Cianciolo, 1976). Artists must understand not only the authors' words, but their intentions as well. The artists bring stories to life, filling them out in rich detail. Maurice Sendak, who personifies the greatness of the visual text, says that authors ". . . must leave a space in the text so the picture can do the work" (Lorraine, 1980, p.326).

Illustrators choose which scenes to illustrate and how to go about it. The choice of subject matter, use of artistic elements, and emphasis on or omission of certain subjects creates a visual text with a message complementary to that of the text.

Illustrations must be consistent with the story in order to enhance communication. The picture must have clear content and form; it should not puzzle the reader (Schulevitz, 1985). William Steig's *Doctor DeSoto* (1982) is an example of a book in which the pictures provide a strong story line. Steig's 31 illustrations depict all the major points and tell a story of a kind-hearted dentist mouse who risks his life to help a fox with a toothache. Silver Burdett & Ginn (Pearson, *et al.*, 1991) uses only five cropped and reduced illustrations. Houghton Mifflin (Pikulski, *et al.*, 1991) uses only ten. Both basal publishers have rendered the illustrations unreadable. They have reduced the book to its written text—it is no longer a picture book. Steig's artistic genius is lost, and the young reader's experience has been drastically changed.

Pacing and Action

Stories consist of many sequences unfolding from beginning to end. Pacing and a clear progression are important, as is action, which moves a story along by introducing characters or elements, or by having a character act on an idea (Roberts, 1981, p.94). Through their uninterrupted sequence, illustrations also tell a story. "[I]llustrations in children's books are a serial art form" (Schwarcz and Schwarcz, 1991, p.5).

Pacing and progression are important to the reader making meaning, and a state of "readability" exists when the reader can easily follow the action from one page to the next (Schulevitz, 1985). The better the sequencing, the easier the illustrations are to read. Through the first few pictures, illustrators suggest a set of rules or a "picture code" (Schulevitz, 1985) to help readers build expectations and make predictions, thus helping them to read the rest of the sequence as it unfolds. A well-designed page is like pacing the story with "more simplicity, more verve, clarity, and impact; to give importance to what is important; to eliminate what destroys the freshness, the originality of the page; in other words, to make a page which will be more easily read by the child" (Duvoisin, 1980, p.305).

The progression of illustrations is carefully planned, and clarity of story is achieved when picture sequences have "continuity and make sense" (Schulevitz, 1985, p.18). Deciding to crop, rearrange, or omit one or more is as complex a job as editing the written text is. In either case bad editing can destroy the text. When basal editors delete and rearrange illustrations, they violate the semiotic "code" of the book the artist has carefully created, robbing the readers of the complete progression and disrupting the meaning of the story and making it less interesting and *harder to read* than the original.

Mercer Mayer's wordless picture book *A Boy, a Dog, and a Frog* (1967) tells the story of a young boy going on a frog hunting expedition. The action unfolds with each turn of the page. There is an element of suspense throughout the book because each page offers a new surprise. In the original 32-page tradebook version, there are 26 interior pictures. In the Harcourt Brace Jovanovich (Heald-Taylor, 1991) basal, the story is told in seven pages. Up to four illustrations are placed on a single page, requiring the publisher to number the pictures because the natural progression of the page turn is lost. The basal version interferes with the prediction-making inherent in Mayer's original. Instead of a picture book, we have something more like a comic book.

When basal editors delete and rearrange illustrations, they violate the semiotic "code" of the book the artist has carefully created.

Characterization

Characters in books are given a visual reality by the illustrator, who must create characters who are

Mood may be disrupted by color changes, the addition or deletion of borders, or the reduction of pages.

believable (Ardizzone, 1980). "The picture book writer can pack a lot more action into his words because the illustrator can develop characters in the pictures . . ." (Roberts, 1981, p.96). ". . . pictures seem to be best able to convey complex emotional responses we might identify with by showing other people experiencing them" (Nodelman, 1991, p.19).

In *Miss Rumphius,* Barbara Cooney (1982) tells the story of a woman's life from childhood to old age. The illustrations of the main character show her growing and aging through every page turn. However, both Houghton Mifflin (Durr, 1989b) and Silver Burdett-Ginn (Pearson, 1991) have deleted so many of the illustrations that it is easy for the reader to miss the passage of time and the character's aging.

Mood

Illustrations may reinforce, communicate, or expand the mood of a story. ". . . artists can imply something of the response they desire to a scene by the way they choose to depict it" (Nodelman, 1991, p.18). Their use of the elements of color, space, size, position, line, shape, texture, perspective, light, and dark all have an effect on the mood, setting, relationships, emotion, and feelings portrayed in the story (Lacy, 1986). The kinds of illustrations used for a story affect the reader's feelings about it before a single word is read. They may evoke feelings and images about the reader's experiences (Cianciolo, 1976). Mood may be disrupted by color changes, the addition or deletion of borders, or the reduction of pages.

Through Grandpa's Eyes (MacLachlan, 1980) is a story of a young boy and his blind grandfather. Throughout the story the boy tries to experience everyday things as they must be to his grandfather. The subtle watercolor illustrations show the experiences the boy shares with his grandfather, and along with the quiet text, provide the reader with a sense of their close relationship. The original illustrations by Deborah Rey are framed by a single, unobtrusive, thin, gray line. Houghton Mifflin (Durr, 1989b), however, framed the illustrations with a thick gold line, encased in two thin black lines, which is then surrounded by a half-inch green border and another thin black line. This disturbs the quiet mood of the story.

Scene and Setting

"A story needs a setting . . . as a picture needs a frame" (Roberts, 1981, p.61). The importance of setting and scene development cannot be underestimated. "Because a picture book is a seeing experience, the sense of place is paramount" (Roberts, 1981, p.69). The reader needs to have a sense of time and place to fully understand it. Setting may not be mentioned in the written text, so it is important that it is portrayed by the artist. Illustrations "act as windows on the world" (Goldstone, 1989, p.593), they widen children's horizons, and they make the story more believable.

Though a sense of time and place is paramount to the meaning of many stories, basal editors often cut the pictures that represent the setting or passing of time. In John Steptoe's African tale *Mufaro's Beautiful Daughters* (1987), the artist's exquisite, detailed illustrations complement the text as they develop the setting in a way that words cannot. Houghton Mifflin (Pikulski, 1991b) shows that it expects the words to do most of the work by cutting several of the pictures.

Book Shape and Size

The selection of book shape and size is intentional, important, and integral to the impact of a picture book. Size and shape are given ample consideration because they may emphasize mood or setting, adding greater credibility to the story line (Cianiciolo, 1976). The page is the "stage or screen" upon which the words and pictures appear (Schulevitz, 1985). An upright rectangle guides the eye in a vertical direction. It is ideal for illustrations that involve heights and tall things. A horizontal rectangle guides the eye across a page and is ideal for landscapes, action, and cumulative stories. A square suggests a circular motion, and is often used when lots of different things are happening (Schulevitz, 1985; Ingram, 1987). All these shapes have a different effect on the response of the reader. The wrong shape can take away from the story. Basals force all their selections to fit into a uniform size and shape.

Borders and Frames

When an illustration extends beyond the edge of a page, it is said to bleed. A picture may bleed on one to four sides of a page, and is done to extend the space beyond what is shown in the picture, or to increase the scale of a picture (Shulevitz, 1985). Over a dozen full-page illustrations in *Miss Rumphius* (Cooney, 1982) bleed on three sides. In Houghton Mifflin (Durr, 1989b) and Silver Burdett-Ginn (Pearson, 1991) this occurs only once.

Other pictures are framed by the white margins of the paper that they are printed on. Pictures and text may also be framed by black or colored borders. These borders vary in thickness and may be made of simple lines or intricate designs. In *A Boy, a Dog, and a Frog* (Mayer, 1967), the pencil illustrations are on completely white pages, surrounded by a thin black line. In the Silver Burdett-Ginn basal (Pearson, 1991) the black lines have been removed and what remains of the white background is placed against a solid yellow background.

Other illustrations are framed by their own edges, the shape of the picture dictating the shape of the white space (Shulevitz, 1985). John Steptoe (1987) used this kind of framing for several of his illustrations, but Houghton Mifflin (Pikulski, 1991b) frequently deleted it.

It is typical of most picture books to have illustrations that occur before or after the actual story.

The Cover and Other Special Pages

Picture books are designed as a whole to achieve a unified impression from cover to cover. It is typical of most picture books to have illustrations that occur before or after the actual story. These illustrations may be found on the cover, half-title page, copyright and dedication page, title page, tail piece, and end papers. The illustrator may choose to begin to tell the story in these early pages. "The cover . . . is like a poster that reflects the mood, text, and artistic style to be found within" (Lacy, 1986, p.7). These pictures on the cover and front matter serve to grab the reader's attention. They cause readers to wonder about the story. They provide clues about what is inside, thus spurring the reader to make predictions.

By choosing to begin the telling of the story through illustration before the print text actually begins, the illustrators get the readers involved in constructing meaning before they even have a chance to see the printed text. The last page in a picture book provides a sense of closure. Sometimes this picture answers the question, "Then what happened?" In virtually every selection, however, these important illustrations are omitted from the basal versions.

Text and Illustration Placement

In a picture book, the amount of text to appear on each page and the way it is arranged is carefully planned to create a balance between print and pictures (Roberts, 1981; Ingram, 1987) and to combine the storytelling powers of the print and pictures. Their placement causes readers to pause in specific places by directing their eyes up or down, left or right, or by a page turn.

Heath (Alvermann, 1991a) considerably rearranged the illustrations and text in *Just Like Daddy* (Asch, 1981), in which the reader is taken through the day of a small bear who does things just like his daddy. The author follows a consistent pattern throughout the book that uses pairs of double-page spreads. The first spread offers two illustrations of the little bear engaged in an activity and the text describing his action. When the reader turns the page, the predictable refrain "Just like Daddy" appears with a single large illustration of the little bear and his daddy. In the basal, however, these sequences of three pictures are placed on one double-page spread, cutting the number of pages used in half.

Picture Composition

Composition and space, or the way that all the picture's elements are organized into a unified whole, are as important to a book's design as the objects portrayed in the illustrations. The positioning of characters and objects helps explain relationships and provides significant insights into a story as well as identify dominant and subordinate characters (Goldstone, 1989). Breathing space (Schulevitz, 1985) is equally important to readability. In picture books, white space is used to emphasize or de-emphasize the print or illustrations, frame illustrations, or to provide logical breaks in the story, yet basal editors treat this spacing as unimportant. They rearrange the print and illustrations for reasons that are not always apparent, the main criterion seeming to be fitting the whole text into the allotted pages. They often ignore logical and significant breaks and pauses as they delete and rearrange illustrations, changing the natural pacing of a story, and in so doing, altering the experiences readers will have with it.

In the original version of *Animals Should Definitely Not Wear Clothing* by Judi Barrett (1970), large text appears on one page, with the appropriate picture by Ron Barrett on the next. This placement invites the reader to pore over the pictures, soak in the details, and enjoy the humor of the story. Heath (Alvermann, 1991b) reduced the story to one double-page spread in which all the illustrations appear simultaneously with the text.

We did not find a single example of a basal in which the font of the original book was retained for either titles or text.

Typestyle

The typeface and typesize should work well with both the story and the illustrations. It should not distract from the whole, but instead enhance the story and mood, usually by being inconspicuous (Shulevitz, 1985). "Typeface must be in harmony, not only with artistic style demonstrated in the pictures, but also with the formal or informal literacy style itself" (Lacy, 1986, p.8). It should also be compatible with the style and color of the illustrations (Cianciolo, 1976). The choice of typeface, then, is an important part of the artistic design of a book. It is a contributor to the overall aesthetic effect.

Typefaces, or fonts, range in style, boldness, and thickness. They may convey formality, informality, brashness, elegance, rusticness, antiquity, cuteness, simplicity, ornateness, and many other moods. Titles are often done in a typeface different from the text. Basals settle for sameness and uniformity; a single font is used for all selections in a given anthology. We did not find a single example of a basal in which the font of the original book was retained for either titles or text.

LOOK WHAT THEY'VE DONE TO POOR IRA

To give a better sense of what happens to a picture book when it is incorporated into a basal, we'll compare the original version of the popular and well-loved picture book *Ira Sleeps Over* written and illustrated by Bernard Waber (1972) with a basal version (1989). Ironically, both versions were published by Houghton Mifflin. *Ira Sleeps Over* is a story of a young boy going to spend the night with a friend for the first time. He wants to take his teddy bear, but is afraid he'll seem babyish. At the end, the reader discovers that Ira's friend also sleeps with a teddy bear. This is a good example of a picture book designed to be easily read by beginning readers. There is nothing artificial about the language, but it is kept simple, even minimal, because so much of the meaning and support is in the pictures.

The written text has not been edited in the basal version: it is there word for word. The changes are all in the pictures and in the related use of space. The original book is 48 pages long. The basal version is 21 pages. There is substantially more text on each page and the twenty selected pictures, all of which are cropped, are not in the same relationship to the writing as in the original.

There is an important loss of meaning in the setting, mood, characterization, and detail of the original and the story is less interesting. One particular example of the cropping in the basal version's illustrations raises questions about the editors' intent: was it to save space or were they censoring the pictures? In the original, there is a wonderfully busy page (see Figure 1). The only text, which takes up just a small amount of space on the bottom of the page, says "We decided to play 'office' with the rubber stamps." It's the kind of page a young reader would spend a lot of time exploring. In the basal version, however, everything but the boys at the table is cropped out (see Figure

We decided to play "office" with the rubber stamps.

Figure 1

2), and both this line and the text from the following several pages appears over the truncated image:

> We decided to play "office" with the rubber stamps.
> After that we had a wrestling match.
> And after that we had a pillow fight.

(In the original, these last two lines are the only print on a page that depicts a pillow fight, complete with flying feathers.)

After that Reggie's father said:

(In the original this line stands by itself in the middle of a blank right-hand page.)

"Bedtime!"

(That's the only word on the page; the illustration in the original shows a very annoyed father and makes it clear that what follows is an argument about going to bed.)

> "Already?" said Reggie.
> "Already," said his father.
> We got into bed.
> "Good night," said Reggie's father.
> "Good night," we said.
> Reggie sighed.
> I sighed.

The dialogue about going to bed is a wonderful example of how rich, inclusive illustrations can minimize the need for print. Young readers can read from the father's face that he has reached the end of his tolerance. In the basal version, were the editors deliberately censoring some of the potentially controversial childish play?

An earlier part of the story in the original takes five

We decided to play "office" with the rubber stamps.

After that we had a wrestling match.

And after that we had a pillow fight.

And after that Reggie's father said:

"Bedtime!"

"Already?" said Reggie.

"Already," said his father.

We got into bed.

"Good night," said Reggie's father.

"Good night," we said.

Reggie sighed.

I sighed.

Figure 2

pages to tell. One page is devoted to a full-page picture; the text in the upper left corner reads:

"Take him," said my mother.
"Take him," said my father.

Mother is sitting on a couch, engrossed in a newspaper, and father is equally preoccupied with the base violin he is playing. Neither looks at Ira as they respond (see Figure 3). In the lower right Ira is saying:

"But Reggie will laugh," I said.
"He'll say I'm a baby."

We get a subtle feeling of pathos and humor at their laid-back attitude, but after a page turn, the reader discovers that they do care. In the illustration, both look up from their occupations to add:

"He won't laugh," said my mother.
"He won't laugh," said my father.

In the basal version (see Figure 4), one page with thirteen lines of text deals with Ira's seeking advice from his family:

Suppose I just hate sleeping without my teddy bear?
Should I take him?
"Take him," said my mother.
"Take him," said my father.
"But Reggie will laugh," I said. "He'll say I'm a baby."
"He won't laugh," said my mother.
"He won't laugh," said my father.
"He'll laugh," said my sister.
I decided not to take my teddy bear.
That afternoon, I played with Reggie.
Reggie had plans, big plans.

Under all the print is a cropped picture of a puzzled Ira sitting in a large wicker chair. Nowhere on this

"Take him," said my mother.
"Take him," said my father.

"But Reggie will laugh," I said.
"He'll say I'm a baby."

Figure 3

Suppose I just hate sleeping without my teddy bear.

Should I take him?

"Take him," said my mother.

"Take him," said my father.

"But Reggie will laugh," I said. "He'll say I'm a baby."

"He won't laugh," said my mother.

"He won't laugh," said my father.

"He'll laugh," said my sister.

I decided not to take my teddy bear.

That afternoon, I played with Reggie. Reggie had plans, big plans.

Figure 4

page or anywhere else does the print establish any characterization for Ira's parents or his relationship with them. Did the editors avoid problems with critics who might have been offended by Ira's slightly unconventional family by leaving the pictures out?

Even the use of space is strikingly different between the two versions. In the original, the line "I decided not to take my teddy bear" is isolated, with a picture of Ira, fist clenched and frowning. In the basal, the line is lost in the block of text surrounding it, and with it is lost the sense of Ira's emotion as he makes his decision.

Obviously the basalization of Ira starts from the need to fit a 48-page picture book into both the physical and instructional constraints of the anthology. However, the basal anthology is not simply a collection of literature. It constitutes a series of texts intended to be used in *teaching children to read*, and this goal is made apparent in the accompanying workbook and teacher's manual. The experiences the children have with the story are controlled by the scope and sequence charts, the skill and word exercises, and the lesson designs superimposed on them. At no time, if the teacher follows the lesson plan, will the children be able to experience the story as a whole, turning the pages and relating the pictures to the print narrative. Whatever the basal editors' purpose for these changes was, without all the pictures and the original arrangement of illustrations and text, it is not the same story.

CONCLUSION

The basals we examined have not maintained the integrity of picture books as an art form or as a genre of literature as they were fit into basal constraints. By violating the relationships of illustrations and print, basal publishers have produced something quite different from the picture books they began with.

Through reducing, deleting, cropping, and rearranging the illustrations, basal publishers have significantly interfered with the support that illustrations provide readers.

In many of the original books we examined, the illustrations were powerful enough to enable children to comprehend the story with a reduced need to rely on the print. They could predict the written text from cues in the pictures. Through reducing, deleting, cropping, and rearranging the illustrations, basal publishers have significantly interfered with the support that illustrations provide readers, forcing them to rely on the printed text to construct meaning. That is probably their intent, but in doing so they have transformed the genre and made the selections more difficult to read than the originals. Once again, in the name of instruction, authentic literature is rendered inauthentic and harder to read by the process of basalization.

Either editors do not understand how children need and use pictures and print to read picture books, or they have quite deliberately chosen to change the fundamental nature of picture books when putting them in the basals. Though it appears they are not sensitive, we believe that basal editors and authors are well-informed about the essential characteristics of picture books as both art form and genre, and therefore, that the transformation of picture books in basals is quite deliberate. Basal publishers have made a choice to make picture books fit their physical and instructional constraints regardless of the effect on the books. It is the only decision they can make given the constraints they have created for themselves. They choose the integrity of the basal over the integrity of the literature.

4

RHYMING WITHOUT REASON: POETRY IN BASALS

DEBBIE BIRDSEYE

> Poetry can—
> make you chuckle,
> or laugh, or cry,
> make you dance
> or shout or sigh.
> Lee Bennett Hopkins

Poetry is important. It appeals to both the thoughts and feelings of its readers, and it offers its writers a chance to express themselves in ways that no other genre can. It has the power to evoke images and deep emotional responses as well as to relate the most cerebral of messages. It invites readers to participate in the poet's experience, no matter what age. Those experiences can emanate from twelve-year-old boys who live in the desert in Arizona, from mothers struggling to raise their children in trailer parks in New Hampshire, and all other people geographically and

Schools have not always been successful when trying to show students the importance of poetry.

culturally in between. However, "poetry can only happen when the poem and the reader connect" (Huck, 1976, p.310).

Schools have not always been successful when trying to show students the importance of poetry. Often poetry has been a forgotten genre, lost between the nursery rhymes of preschool and the sonnets of Shakespeare in secondary school. This neglect denies children the opportunity of coming to know themselves and their world in poetic ways.

In an effort to help elementary school children learn to appreciate and use poetry, basal publishers have included poetry in their anthologies. Poet Georgia Heard (1989) cautions that "the reading and writing of poetry must begin with the joy of it" (p.8). I examined recent editions of Harcourt, Brace, Jovanovich (Heald-Taylor *et al.*, 1989), Heath (Alvermann *et al.*, 1991), Macmillan (Arnold, *et al.*, 1990), and Silver Burdett-Ginn (Pearson *et al.*, 1991) in order to determine whether or not students' basal experiences with poetry begin with joy.

BASAL POETRY

Poetry is included in basals in several ways: as a part of a theme study, unit or cluster, as an add-on to a story, as a subject of genre study, as a introduction to a unit, or as a text for teachers to share orally with their students. Not all the poetry that appears in basals is listed in the table of contents of the anthologies, making it difficult to assess just how much poetry students might experience. Rarely are poems allowed to stand alone as texts worthy of reading for their own sake. Rather, more often than not, poems are connected to other texts thematically, thus limiting the types of responses the poems can evoke. And in fact, poetry occurs rarely in most basals. For example, at the first-grade level, Harcourt Brace Jovanovich includes thirteen poems, Heath includes three, Macmillan four, and Silver Burdett-Ginn six. This means that students reading through Heath will encounter

one poem every thirteen weeks, while students reading Harcourt Brace Jovanovich must only wait an average of three weeks.

*Poetry occurs
rarely in most
basals.*

These encounters are seldom joyous occasions. For
example, "Rainbow Days" is a selection of two American Indian poems published in a first-grade Harcourt
Brace Jovanovich anthology. They appear in the
teacher's manual like this:

Rainbow Days
Two American Indian Poems

In summer the rains come,
The grass grows up,
and the deer has new horns.
—A Yaqui poem

You, whose day it is,
Make it beautiful.
Get out your rainbow colors,
So it will be beautiful.
—A Nootka poem

172

173

Figure 1

The Yaqui poem was originally published in *Songs
of the Dream People,* edited by James Houston (1972).
It is one of the deer songs of the Yaqui people. The
Yaqui Indians have an annual springtime ceremony
that includes the deer dance performed to deer songs.
These songs are highly stylized and usually sung by
three men while dancers symbolize connections between the spiritual and natural worlds. Although this
information is germane to the oral interpretation and
understanding of the poem, the teacher's manual
does not mention its significance to Yaqui culture.

Rudine Sims Bishop (1982) suggests that multicultural children's literature should provide the opportunity for readers to see and better understand other cultures. However, without any information on the relevance of deer songs, neither the poem nor the multicultural experience is realized.

Not only is relevant cultural information withheld, but the translation and companion illustration offer misinformation. The illustration pictures a deer in a meadow with mesas in the background. Northern Mexico and southern Arizona, the land of the Yaqui, have neither mesas nor meadows like the one shown in the illustration. Second, deer do not have horns; they have antlers that can be shed each year because they are not a permanent part of the animal's bone structure.

Beyond the factual and cultural misinformation, students are invited to experience the poems in the following way (Figure 2). But this is just the beginning.

Figure 2

The teacher's manual offers a vast array of activities to accompany these seven lines of text (Figure 3).

These activities are to be spread over a five-day period. On day one, the teacher is to prepare the students to read the poem, and then read it. On day two,

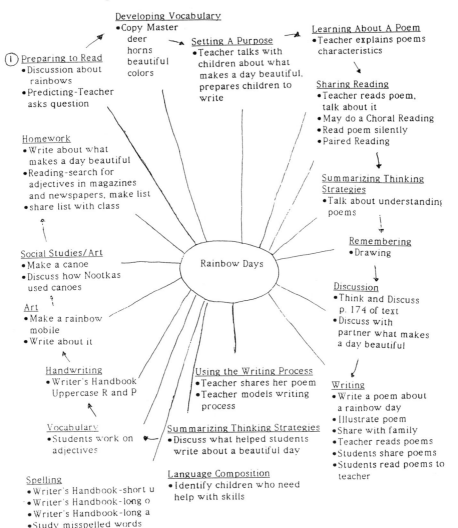

Figure 3

the students remember the selection and discuss it. Students are to work independently on days three and four, doing the various skill exercises. And on day five, they extend the poems into art and social studies by making rainbow mobiles and paper canoes.

In the student anthology, the poems are preceded by two pages of text that get them to focus on "Rainbow Days" before they read it. Students are encouraged to discuss their experiences with rainbows and predict what a rainbow day might be. In the teacher's manual, teachers are introduced to the lesson: "While reading the poems, children will focus on the beauty of nature. Children will also use writing, listening, and speaking skills as they respond to the selection. They will use higher-level thinking skills as they discuss and write" (p.258). These skills are encoded in 27 objectives for the five days. In all, fifteen pages in the teacher's manual are devoted to the explanation of how to help students experience these two poems.

Part of this experience requires students to write poems individually, keeping their families in mind as an audience and following a prewriting, drafting, responding, revising, editing, evaluating, and post-writing sequence as they do. The teacher's manual asks the teacher to model this sequence and supplies an example poem as if the teacher wrote it:

> On a rainbow day,
> The sun shines through the trees,
> Flowers open their petals,
> And I get hugs.

Questions and expected responses are provided for the teacher to model revision for her students (p.264):

> Did I tell what makes a Rainbow Day beautiful? (Yes, I wrote about the sun shining, flowers blooming, and hugs.)

Did I tell enough about a Rainbow Day? (No, I forgot to tell how I could make the day beautiful. I will add I smile at everyone after the third line.)
What can I do to make my writing more interesting? (I can add describing words. I will add the words bright before sun, beautiful before flowers, and warm before hugs in the third line.)

Finally, there are twelve pages of workbook and worksheets for students to complete. The following pages come from the student's Writer's Handbook.

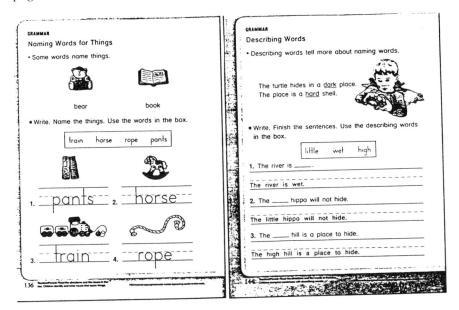

Figure 4

While I am certain that the suggestions to teachers are intended to be helpful, I am not certain what any of them have to do with the poems. Clearly, the publishers did not intend to offend the Yaqui people or to force teachers to lie to their students, but they did intend to bury these poems in an avalanche of skills and activities that can do little more than confuse

The skills emphasis also effects students' stances while they read the poems.

young readers about the power and possibilities of poetry.

This focus on skills extends beyond first grade and Harcourt Brace Jovanovich. For example, "This Tooth," a poem by Lee Bennett Hopkins, follows a play called "The Huge Toothache" in Macmillan's third-grade anthology. These selections are part of a unit called All About Me, which focuses on personal health. At the beginning of the unit there are no objectives listed about health, plays, or poetry. The stated objectives include decoding and phonics skills, comprehension and vocabulary skills, and study skills. This focus on skills is presented to teachers as an imperative:

> Tell children that some poems have rhyming words and some do not. As them to listen as you read the poem aloud.
> Are there any words that rhyme? (Yes.) Which words rhyme? (Alone, own) (p.175).

The skills emphasis also effects students' stances while they read the poems and their responses to the poem after having done so. For example, consider the directions to teachers concerning the reading and interpretation of "The Baker," a poem by Arnold Adoff, published in the Heath fifth-grade anthology, and those from "Secret Talk," a poem by Eve Merriam, published in the Silver Burdett-Ginn third-grade anthology.

> Have students read the poem silently to find out what this baker bakes. Discuss the poem, then assign lines and have the students give a choral reading of the poem.
> INFERENTIAL: What does this baker bake? (pizza)
> LITERAL: According to the baker, what is the most important ingredient in this pizza? Why do you think

the baker feels this way? (The dough because that's
the part he made; everything else rests on the dough)
CRITICAL/CREATIVE: Look at the unusual way the
words in the poem are arranged. What does this arrangement of words suggest to you? (Students might
suggest that the words are layered in the same way
the toppings on pizza might be.) (Heath, p.110)

INTRODUCING THE POEM (Secret Talk)
RELATE CONTENT OF THE POEM TO STUDENTS'
EXPERIENCE.
Ask student if they have ever spent time with a close
friend but not talked for periods of time. Point out
that good friends often do not have to speak a word
to communicate because they know about each other
and feel comfortable with each other.
SET A LISTENING PURPOSE.
Tell students they are going to hear a poem about two
friends who meet and spend time together. Ask them
to think about the poet's message.
DISCUSS STUDENTS' RESPONSES TO THE POEM.
Ask students if the poem gives them a feeling of excitement or a quiet feeling and why. (quiet feeling
because the friends do not speak and their activities
are quite) Then ask: By telling how the friends spend
a day, what is the poet's message about friendship?
(friends know what each other enjoys doing and the
enjoy doing many of these things together.)
WHAT MESSAGE DO YOU GET FROM THE POET'S
WORDS "SECRET TALK"? (Friends can talk without
speaking, and what they say is a secret they share)
(Silver Burdett-Ginn, p.265)

Arnold Adoff said, "I really want a poem to sprout
roses and spit bullets" (Hopkins, 1987), and Eve Merriam suggested that poems are mysteries to be addressed by all readers who come to the poem (Huck,
1976). Do the purposes set and the questions asked
in these teacher's manuals allow Adoff's poem to
sprout or spit? Do they honor Merriam's mysterious
secret? They do not. Rather they treat the poems as

In basals, neither teachers nor students are encouraged to adopt an aesthetic stance while reading poems.

if they were statements of fact to be picked apart matter-of-factly. This treatment reduces the student/reader's possible stances and interpretation to the impoverished ones of basal publishers. "Textbooks' and teachers' questions too often hurry the student away from the lived-through experience. After the reading, the experience should be recaptured, reflected on" (Rosenblatt, 1991, p.447).

Telling a purpose for reading or suggesting that there is "a" point to any poem does not leave room for students to consider the possibility that there may be more that one point or that each reader may find his or her own points or interpretations. "Aesthetic reading happens if students have repeatedly found that in approaching a text called a poem or story, they can assume that they are free to pay attention to what the words call to consciousness. They can savor the images, the sounds, the smell, the actions, the associations, and the feelings that the words point to" (Rosenblatt, 1991, p.447).

POETRY AS CHOICE

Poetry is present in new basals; however, its unique qualities of images, sounds, textures, rhythms, and richness seem to be overlooked and underappreciated. In basals, neither teachers nor students are encouraged to adopt an aesthetic stance while reading poems. This seems tragic because, of all the genres, poetry is known for being able to be appreciated from an aesthetic stance. Unfortunately, this approach may not be possible given the nature of basals.

The editors who select the poems to be included in the anthologies cannot know the individual classroom communities, the students, or the teachers who will use their wares. They do not know the interests, language, culture, background experiences, or concerns and joys of specific classes. It is a basic and insurmountable problem inherent in basals. Because they serve an abstract national market and because they are constructed to teach reading skills, basals cannot provide the poetry that will speak powerfully to the individuals who must use them.

Perhaps more than other genres, poetry requires a sensitive teacher who with insight, intuition, knowledge, and involvement with living individuals and groups of students on a daily basis can find the special poems that will help students to appreciate and use poetry. Only teachers can identify the poetry that will be meaningful to themselves and their students. As Lee Bennett Hopkins (1987) suggests:

> There is really little difference between good poetry for children and good poetry for adults. Poetry for children should appeal to them and meet their emotional needs and interests. We can read about what poetry or a poem is, what it should do, learn all about meters, rhyme schemes, cadence, and balance; yet all this does not necessarily help to make a poem meaningful. The one criterion we must set for ourselves is that we love the poems we are going to share. If we don't like a particular poem, we shouldn't read it to our children; our distaste will certainly be obvious to them. There are plenty of poems around. Why bother with those that are not pleasing? (p.9)

There is little joy or anything pleasing in the way that basals present and treat poetry.

5

STEP ONE, STEP TWO, STEP THREE, FOUR, FIVE, MY, THIS WRITING SEEMS CONTRIVED! WRITING PROCESS IN BASAL READING PROGRAMS

LISA BURLEY MARAS

Schools are putting an increased emphasis on writing, and many of the "new" basals are responding to this increased emphasis by claiming to integrate writing into their programs. This is evident in the new basals' frequent use of many currently popular terms in their teacher's manuals and in their promotional material. Terms such as "holistic," "literature-based," "integrated across the curriculum," "beyond the basal," and "writing process," among others, are frequently used to describe their philosophy and program. However, some of the claims that these "new" basals are making in regard to the teaching of writing need to be examined.

These teachers recognize the need for children to have multiple opportunities to be engaged in purposeful, meaningful, relevant, writing.

WRITING PROCESS

Writing is one of our most important forms of communication. We write for many reasons: to relay messages, share ideas, request information, complain, send wishes, remember, entertain, inform, and for our own pleasure. Researchers such as Denny Taylor and Shirley Brice Heath have helped us understand the many functions of writing, the reasons we write, and the form that writing takes. Other researchers have helped teachers understand the processes that readers and writers go through. Significant research in reading and writing processes by people such as Nancie Atwell, Lucy Calkins, Ken Goodman, Yetta Goodman, Donald Graves, Frank Smith, and many others has given teachers more information, insight, and understanding into the way children learn to read and write.

Change in the Classroom

Many teachers are applying research about the writing process to their teaching, thus changing their classroom practice. They know that children learn to read in supportive, literate environments where they are surrounded by books, immersed in writing of all kinds, and are involved in authoring (Goodman, 1986). These teachers recognize the need for children to have multiple opportunities to be engaged in purposeful, meaningful, relevant, writing. In these classrooms, children use writing to communicate with others, express themselves, and as a tool for reflection and learning about themselves and the world around them. Writing process teachers know that "writing both fosters understanding and expresses it" (Weaver, 1990, p.179).

Process

Beyond the forms of writing, teachers understand the writing process so that they can help students use, adapt, and invent strategies for effective writing (Calkins, 1986). The writing process is described using various terms: prewriting, brainstorming, drafting, rehearsing, writing, composing, rewriting, conferencing, revising, proofreading, editing, and publishing, among others. The terms used are not as important as the understanding that the writing process is recursive, not linear, and allows the writer to circle out and circle back (Calkins, 1986).

Although writers may use similar approaches, their journey through the writing process will differ. Successful writers do what is most pertinent and helpful at a given time for a particular purpose. How they go through the process reflects differences in personality, preference, style, function, and purpose. In order for writing to be facilitated, successful, and meaningful, writers must have time to write, have ownership over their writing, and receive responses from those around them (Atwell, 1987).

When writing is given time and priority, students are able to develop the habits of writers (Calkins, 1986).

Time, Ownership, and Response

When writing is given time and priority, students are able to develop the habits of writers (Calkins, 1986). When provided with time they can count on, children begin to take control of their own writing. They develop strategies as they learn to make decisions about when to draft, revise, confer, or put a piece aside. Donald Murray (Calkins, 1991, p.229) says that writers need "time for staring out of windows, time for thinking, time for dreaming, time for doodling, time for rehearsing, planning, drafting . . . circling, moving closer, backing off, coming at it from a different angle, circling again, trying a new approach." It is important to remember that good writing takes time. Having the opportunity to make decisions about their writing helps students to take ownership of the writing process. Writing should always serve a real purpose or need to communicate on the part of the writer. It should be relevant to their lives, and reflect their needs, interests, and experiences. The writer must be in control of the process and its use (Goodman, *et al.*, 1987).

The ability to choose topic and genre, the what and how of writing, allows the writer's voice to be heard. Graves (1983) says it is our own voice that provides us with the reason for writing in the first place. We write because we have something to say and a need or reason for saying it. Children need to have opportunities to listen, talk, and respond with and to their teachers and peers. When sharing time is provided, children are able to share their creations and also talk about their process (Harste, Short, and Burke, 1988). They can discuss problems, offer suggestions, ask questions, and provide support. Children need an audience when they are writing. This helps them to think through and about their writing (Weaver, 1990). Atwell (1987) reminds us that children need to be responded to while they are immersed in their writing, while they are in the process, not when they are finished. By having opportunities to share their writing with an audience they learn the value of supporting ideas, sequencing, providing details, legibility, and more.

Conversations between writers are fundamental to the writing process. When teachers conference with their students they are trying to help them find what they want to say, and also help them to say it well (Calkins, 1986). Writing process teachers are concerned with form and clarity, as well as the skills of punctuation, spelling, capitalization, and more. But these teachers also know that it is worthless to concentrate on the technical aspects of writing if children have not had the chance to "just write" about the things that really matter in their lives.

WHAT THE PROGRAM AUTHORS SAY ABOUT WRITING PROCESS AND THE WRITING PROCESS EXPERIENCES BASALS PROVIDE

Houghton Mifflin

Houghton Mifflin (1989a) claims that the writing projects provided in their program are based on the writing process. Houghton Mifflin further asserts that their writing projects "exercise student's creativity and critical thinking skills" (1989a, p.21). In their Selection Plans book (1989b) they state that they provide writing process opportunities with each reading selection. They model topic selection, planning, draft preparation, revision, proofreading, and publishing (1989b). They say that they incorporate peer evaluation and cooperative learning.

Houghton Mifflin also offers "how-to" masters to assist students in completing writing activities independently (1989a). They provide instruction in mechanics, spelling, grammar, and usage.

Houghton Mifflin presents the writing process in a five-step, linear sequence in each lesson, for each grade level: Step 1—Prewriting; Step 2—Write a first draft; Step 3—Revise; Step 4—Proofread; and Step 5—Publish. A writing process lesson sequence from the first grade manual (1989b, p.139–140) involves children in writing a complete story. In this example, the teacher reminds the students about a story that they read. The teacher then tells the children that they will write their own stories about one of the characters—a fox—and what he could do to find food. Five-step directions are provided for the teacher.

Step 1—Prewriting: The teacher directs a discussion on settings for their stories. After this discussion,

Houghton Mifflin presents the writing process in a five-step, linear sequence in each lesson, for each grade level.

children are directed to write their story about a place where the fox would go to eat.

Step 2—Write a First Draft: Children are directed to begin their stories by copying a sentence provided in the teacher's manual. The teacher is then directed to ask a list of supplied questions to help them write. The teacher is told to pause after each question so that children can print their answers.

Step 3—Revise: The teacher asks the children to read their stories. Questions are again provided so that the teacher can suggest additions and changes.

Step 4—Proofread: Children are told to reread their stories and correct any mistakes they may have made. They are told to make sure words are spelled correctly, and to check that each sentence begins with a capital and ends with punctuation.

Step 5—Publish: Children are told to copy their stories onto clean paper, and are encouraged to illustrate them. The manual says that the stories should be bound into a book entitled *The Further Adventures of the Hungry Fox,* and are to be displayed in the reading corner or classroom library.

Although students are taken through the whole process and complete a whole story, this lesson infringes on many things we know about writing, but perhaps none more than ownership. The topic is dictated by the manual, the first sentence of the story is provided, and a series of questions for students to answer decides the details and sequence of the story. Even the type and title of publication is given.

This lesson provides an inauthentic and simplistic approach to story writing. Stories do not begin with a line provided by someone else, nor are they developed by answering a series of questions. Harste, Short, and Burke say "When we write, the text is never wholly conceived beforehand" (1988, p.10). It is created and recreated as we think, stop, ponder, read, talk, write, reflect, wonder, and so on. In this lesson the text has already been written by the program, and every story has an invariant form.

D.C. Heath

D.C. Heath Reading states that their program "mirrors natural writing processes," and claims to teach a "whole process approach to writing" (1993a, p.41). Heath mentions that research into what authors do has been translated into valuable classroom practices. They represent the writing process in these stages: prewriting, writing, revising, editing, and postwriting. They say that the stages may overlap, be repeated, or may be skipped entirely (1991, p.5).

Heath says that learning to write is important because ". . . it helps children organize and express their thoughts" (1993a, p.41). Heath considers both reading and writing to be part of the same thinking process and mutually enhancing. ". . . reading improves writing and writing improves reading" (1991, p.4). So Heath intergrates writing activities throughout the readings (1991, p.5), and offers lessons for direct instruction in the writing process. They go on to say that when they focus on specific parts of the process for direct instruction, it is always done in the context of the whole process (1993a, p.41).

Throughout the grade levels, each Heath lesson is divided into four sections: 1) Link; 2) Learn; 3) Practice; and 4) Apply. This example from Heath Reading (1993b, p.37–39), Grade 5, represents a sequence of three writing process lessons.

1) Link: The lesson begins with the teacher asking students two questions as supplied in the manual in order to link letter writing to a previously read selection. The teacher is told to explain to students that "since a letter represents the writer, it is important that it communicate its message well." The objective of this lesson is to review the elements of writing ef-

fective letters. The teacher is directed to display and review the five steps in the writing process if necessary.

2) Learn: To review steps in prewriting, the teacher is told to explain that before beginning a letter there are important questions that must be answered. Six questions are provided for the teacher to ask, and students are asked to answer them as the main character in the story might have.

3) Practice: Students are coached through prewriting as the teacher is told to tell everyone that they will work through the prewriting portion of the writing plan and then check the plan with a classmate before writing. A workbook page is provided to assist to this end. The teacher is directed to explain that for this exercise, "they will plan a letter to a newspaper or magazine telling their opinions about a local problem."

The teacher is told to remind students to consider who their audience is and to record it on the workbook page or paper. The teacher is told to give students time to brainstorm local problems and to write these suggestions on the board. Students are then told to record their choice on the workbook page or paper.

Students are given a few minutes to consider their feelings about the problem and are asked to consider possible solutions to the problem. Once they have recorded this information they are told to discuss their prewriting plans with classmates and revise accordingly.

4) Apply: Students are told to write a rough draft of the letter to a newspaper or magazine. They are reminded to think about the form, including the correct salutation and closing, before they begin to write. They are then told to save the letter in their writing portfolios. During a different lesson, (1993b, p.80–81) this letter is pulled out in order to be revised.

1) Link: The teacher displays a letter and asks for reactions.

2) Learn: The teacher reviews five elements of revising provided in the manual. The letter on display is analyzed using the five criteria, and the group is told to brainstorm how they could change the letter.

3) Practice: The teacher divides students into small groups so that they can rewrite the letter using the five criteria. A workbook page is also provided to give students additional practice in revising a letter to eliminate irrelevant details.

4) Apply: Students are told to apply the five criteria to revise the letters they wrote to a newspaper or magazine. They are told to exchange rough drafts, and give suggestions for revision. They are told to return the letters to their writing portfolios. In the next lesson (1993b, p.120–123), this letter is pulled out again, this time to be edited.

1) Link: The lesson begins by focusing on spelling errors. The teacher is provided a sentence with a spelling error to write on the board. The teacher reminds students that "our writing reveals more about us than we realize" and that "we must be sure that our ideas are clear and that errors do not weaken the forcefulness of our message." The teacher reviews the writing process with a focus on editing.

2) Learn: The teacher reminds students that when they are editing, they are correcting mistakes in grammar, spelling, punctuation, and capitalization. The teacher then points out that pronoun usage is a part of grammar. Using sentences from the manual that contain pronoun errors the teacher reviews pronoun usage.

3) Practice: The teacher displays a paragraph with several pronoun errors. Students edit the paragraph. They are then given a workbook page for additional editing practice.

4) Apply: Students are told to exchange papers and edit each other's work, focusing especially on pronoun usage.

This sequence of lessons provides a complete look

Heath's lessons do not demonstrate a recursive writing process as claimed.

at the total writing process experience that Heath provides. Heath's lessons do not demonstrate a recursive writing process as claimed. Each lesson leads to the next step.

It is clear that writing is not the focus of these lessons. Although Heath claims that they always address the whole writing process in context, it is the "skills" of letter writing, editing, spelling, and pronoun usage that drive these lessons. The letter is just a means to these ends. Students use contrived paragraphs and workbook pages to practice skills before they get to their own writing. Although there are opportunities for students to work together, it is to correct, not respond, to each other. In both texts the focus of editing is on correctness, not content.

As teachers, we have to remember that the pieces our students are writing are not ours, and that they are ultimately responsible for making the decisions about their writing. Although writing process teachers often discuss the technical elements of genre, tense, punctuation, editing, and other "skills," they do so with real pieces of writing, when it is most relevant. They prepare lessons based on students' questions and needs. We may make suggestions, but when we take control of the process, we have taken the ownership of the piece from the writer.

The authors of the basal programs have taken control away from the writer. They have chosen the skills to be learned. Heath considers writing a "way of creating new ideas and clarifying information" (1991, p.4). However, in these lessons children are not involved in creating new ideas, they are creating what the program tells them to. It is interesting to note that there is never any mention of actually sending these letters out to a newspaper or magazine. This letter is one of many examples of unmotivated, unfinished, and abandoned pieces throughout all levels of their program.

Silver Burdett-Ginn

In their teacher's manual, Silver Burdett-Ginn states that "since reading, writing, listening and speaking are interrelated and interdependent, it makes sense to plan language arts experiences that are mutually supportive. . . . Every selection in *World of Reading* has a 'Reading/Writing Connection' with opportunities to integrate the language arts" (1993a, p.M20). Reading and writing are referred to as "partners" in learning, so "writing is employed to help students discover ideas, explore literary relationships, and bond new information to the known." Several writing activities are suggested throughout each unit to involve children in writing.

"Integrating Reading and Writing" is specifically labeled as a writing process activity. This writing process activity is provided at the end of each unit. Children are provided with a Reader's/Writer's Notebook (1993b). These are workbook pages on which students can work through the writing process, either on their own, or during a teacher-directed lesson provided in the manual. Silver Burdett-Ginn names a five-step writing process that includes prewriting, writing, revising, proofreading, and publishing.

In a third-grade lesson from Silver Burdett-Ginn (1993a, p.998–1000), the teacher is directed to begin the lesson by reviewing the unit theme through the use of questions provided in the manual. The teacher then previews the writing assignment by discussing the form of a narrative. The teacher then introduces the writing activity by having students recall details from the stories that they read and to think about how the stories were written to help them come up with ideas for their own stories. Students are told that they will use the writing process to write their own story about a "special weather" day in their life.

The teacher is directed to assist students in setting a purpose for writing that is stated in the manual as "to create a realistic story with a beginning, middle, and end."

Prewriting: The teacher suggests that students discuss questions supplied in the manual with a partner in order to help them choose their topic. They are then given a story chart to complete.

Writing: Students are directed to use the information from their story chart to write a weather story. It is suggested that they begin with a telling sentence. The teacher is directed to remind students to tell events in order, use action verbs, and emphasize that it is important to get ideas, and that they can revise and correct errors later.

Revising: Students are directed to read the story to themselves and to a partner. Questions they should ask each other are supplied.

Proofreading: Students are told to check for errors in spelling, capitalization, and end punctuation. Students are told to review the action verbs in their story to see whether they used action verbs like "twirled" and "pushed" to describe actions clearly.

Publishing: The manual offers three suggestions for sharing stories, including reading it out loud to classmates or making a "True Weather Tales" class book. Children are even given the opportunity to come up with their own publishing ideas.

The questions that teachers ask should urge students to look at their writing in a different way. When we talk to students about revising, we have to help them "re-vision" their piece, to see it again (Heard, 1989). Comments and suggestions should serve to help move them forward in their writing (Atwell, 1987), not simply fulfill the predetermined objectives in a program. The list of questions that are provided in the basal appears to serve as a check to see if lesson objectives were met. Children need to be asked real questions in order to understand the needs of their audience. Teachers and peers should ask questions when they are confused or have a genuine interest.

We need to be wary of questions that are asked solely to spur revision. Our questions should invite writers to talk, elaborate, and clarify so that they may reflect on their own writing (Atwell, 1987).

We need to be wary of questions that are asked solely to spur revision.

Macmillan/McGraw-Hill

In their staff development magazine, *A New View*, Macmillan/McGraw-Hill states that "writing must be an extensive part of the reading program from the very beginning," and that reading and writing are developed concurrently, not sequentially, and reinforce and build on each other (1993a, p.13). Literacy is described as a social activity and it is said that "language skills are best developed collaboratively when students speak and listen to one another, and when teachers build on the language skills that children possess" (1993a, p.26).

Macmillan/McGraw-Hill says that writing process is "best taught by example" (1993b, p.219). They also state in their *Staff Development Guide* (1993b) that writing process is not following a sequence of steps, and that stages may overlap and be repeated.

"From Reading to Writing" is the title of the writing process activities. In all these activities, students are led through a five-step process labeled prewriting, drafting, revising, proofreading, and publishing.

In these lessons, the manual offers three options for the teacher to choose from, based on what the teacher thinks students need. One is a complete writing process lesson. Another reviews a model of the type of writing they will be doing in the lesson. The last provides practice with a writing prompt. For our purposes, a focus on the complete writing process lesson is most appropriate.

All stages of the process begin with a "Think Aloud." The "Think Alouds" are written as complete scripts that provide examples of the kind of modeling the teacher might do (1993d, p.61C). Transparencies are also provided for each stage of the writing process. These transparencies are specific to each "From Reading to Writing" lesson, and provide teachers with questions and another model to stimulate a discussion on the specific step in the process, and to help students get ideas.

A lesson on story writing is provided in the Macmillan/McGraw-Hill third-grade manual (1993d, p.61A–G). The teacher relates the lesson to previous readings about clever characters who solved problems in unusual ways.

Prewriting: The teacher begins with a Think Aloud to model the process of deciding what to write about, and brainstorming words and phrases that come to mind about the topic. The manual states that students can work in small groups to talk about clever and unusual characters who are able to solve problems. Students are told to make a list of story ideas, and check the two or three they find most interesting. Students then brainstorm a purpose, audience, and topic for their story. The teacher points out the value of a preliminary plan for writing, and uses a transparency to model a story organizer. Students can create their own charts in a Literature Activity Book (1993e, p.18).

Drafting: The teacher begins with a Think Aloud to model drafting. Before students are invited to begin their own drafts, the manual suggests that the teacher discuss the key features of writing that entertains. Four criteria are provided. Students are reminded that the purpose of drafting is to capture ideas and not worry about spelling or punctuation. Another transparency is provided to help students think about drafting.

Revising: The teacher models revising through the Think Aloud and a transparency of a revised story. In order to help students "rethink" their own writing, they are told to draw the story in a cartoon strip. They then compare their stories to the illustrations by answering questions such as, "Does my story have a beginning, middle, and an end?" Children are then encouraged to read their drafts to a partner and ask for comments. Questions are provided in a Peer Conferencing Checklist box in the Teacher's Planning Guide, in order to focus students on aspects of story writing.

Proofreading: The focus of the proofreading Think Aloud is on capitalization, run-on sentences, paragraph indentations, and quotation marks. After modeling, the teacher might have students proofread on their own, or may use the transparency in order to review the rules for the conventions mentioned in the Think Aloud.

Publishing: After the teacher models some thoughts on publishing in the Think Aloud, students are invited to discuss their ideas. Some suggestions are provided in the manual. After completing their final copies, students can engage in a self-evaluation activity by comparing their writing to an annotated model in the Writer's Workshop (1993c, p.107), or evaluate another model on the provided transparency.

Macmillan/McGraw-Hill says that writing process is not following a sequence of steps and is taught by example, yet, in their writing process lessons, the teacher models the writing process in a five-step, linear sequence. The modeling in these lessons monopolizes so much time there seems that there could be little left for writing. The modeling also keeps the lessons teacher-centered, thus allowing children only a few, controlled opportunities to work together. This is interesting for a program that says that language skills are best developed when students speak and listen to one another (1993a, p.26).

IS THIS REALLY WRITING PROCESS?

The writers and publishers of these programs have recognized the importance of writing process and

At first glance, it appears that basal reading programs have made substantial changes and improvements.

have made a deliberate attempt to include writing in their newer programs in order to present a balanced, integrated language arts program. At first glance, it appears that basal reading programs have made substantial changes and improvements. However, upon closer examination, it is evident that they have had to alter writing process to fit the constraints of the basal program. Many of the claims that are made in the program overviews are abandoned in the teacher's manuals, where the writing process is reduced to a rigid, linear, five-step, sequence. Superimposed on that is the basal lesson sequence. The focus of these programs continues to be the teaching, reinforcing, and practicing of a sequence of skills that have been arbitrarily chosen by the authors and editors. Writing instruction is used to master and practice these skills, instead of its intended purpose of communication, self-expression, and as a tool for learning about the world around us.

Ownership has been usurped by the program. Teachers are reduced to technicians whose role is to guide students through the program's predetermined sequence. Lessons are scripted and directive and present a regimented, part-to-whole approach to the writing process. The programs control what and how the students write. Students are pushed through a linear, five-step process, working on lessons that are based on the arbitrary decisions of the editorial team, and what they think children should learn. Children write for inauthentic purposes, and spend much of their time writing about things that have no relevance to their lives. The way these programs are organized, it appears that the editorial teams are operating under the assumption that children are incapable of making their own choices in writing, and that they do not have any skills or understandings that have not been explicitly taught by the program. Teachers are regarded as incapable of judging for themselves the needs of their students and lacking in the ability to plan appropriate lessons to support and facilitate writing in their classrooms.

The basal programs do not provide students with the time they need to really develop their pieces, share with others, or reflect on their writing. Writing happens at set intervals, depending on the programs' scope and sequence. Typically, the only audience children write for is the teacher, who is correcting (with directives from the manual), not responding. In the few instances where children are given opportunities to talk to a partner about their writing, the manual directs what the children talk about, and how they go about it. The typical focus of these interactions is not on responding to the writer, but on fixing and correcting mistakes.

The writing lessons in all of these programs are used to teach the explicit sequence of skills, genres, and topics that were chosen to be covered in the program. Often, there are lessons that focus on the direct teaching of the writing process. Specific lessons in drafting, revising, and editing are provided, and are frequently done with inauthentic pieces supplied in the manual. The basal programs are so concerned with making sure children know the parts of the process, or other specific skills, that there is no time left for the children to actually be involved in writing. Writing is secondary to the lesson, it falls by the wayside, and is even forgotten. Accuracy is demanded at all levels of development.

These programs do not reflect our current understanding of writing process. Misunderstandings and misinterpretations are very apparent in all the programs reviewed. The reasons people write, the crucial elements of time, ownership, and response, as well as the recursive, personal, and social nature of the writing process, are absent. These programs are still based on a skills-based, sequenced, part-to-whole, model of learning. The writing lessons are contrived,

Teachers should be working with children to help them get deeper into their writing.

redundant, and inauthentic, making it difficult to facilitate and support children in their writing.

Teachers should be working with children to help them get deeper into their writing, so that it enhances their understanding of themselves and their world. In these programs children are not writing for themselves. They do what is asked, and practice specific skills, such as using pronouns, commas, active verbs, or capitals. Such contrived lessons are not necessary when children are involved in real writing. Weaver suggests that it may not be necessary to teach the skills children need to read and write directly. She says, "wide reading and extensive writing appear to be the key" (Weaver, 1988, p.199). In order to become better writers, children need to be involved in authentic writing every day.

6

PATTERNS OF CULTURE OR DISTORTED IMAGES: MULTICULTURALISM IN BASALS

ELAINE SCHWARTZ

One in four Americans currently belongs to a recognized minority group.

Over the past few years schools have been enmeshed in a national debate over multiculturalism. Recent changes in our country's demographic patterns have brought a certain urgency to this issue for school officials. According to the United States Bureau of the Census one in four Americans currently belongs to a recognized minority group. In the very near future, "in more than 50 cities across the country, public schools will draw students primarily from minority population" (Kabagarama, 1993, p.10). In cities of varying size across the United States, Anglo-Americans are already in the minority (Associated Press, 1993). Thus, multiculturalism as an integral part of American society must also be an integral part of the public school curriculum. Indeed, many state education departments (*e.g.* California, New York, and so on) have policies that require multiculturalism in all aspects of schooling. As a central component of elementary school curriculum, reading lessons should provide children with texts that present their cultures and portray the multicultural web of American society. Publishers of basal reading series have responded to these policies through the inclusion of multicultural children's literature and lessons in their textbooks.

Literature has traditionally been recognized as a way in which readers come to understand themselves and others. "To awaken consciousness, to reveal reality, can literature claim a better function?" (Galeano, 1988, p.119). Novels of initiation (*e.g.*, Mark Twain's *The Adventures of Huckleberry Finn*, or Kate Chopin's *The Awakening*) have been used in schools to help individuals explore their relationships with others and the patterns of values, language, and behavior that comprise the cultures that demarcate social groups. By using characters to place culture in relationships with one another, literature has the potential to help us set our lives in their social contexts and to provide windows through which we can see the lives and the social contexts of others. Literature can provide new knowledge and alternative ways of looking at the world, and it can touch our minds and our hearts, helping us to recognize our unique contribution to society or teaching us that others do not think much of the contributions of our culture or ourselves.

Throughout the history of American schooling, the literature used in classrooms (including basal anthologies) has not been equally affirming for all social groups. In fact, much of it has been racist, sexist, classist, and subject to a variety of biases that affirm white middle and upper class Anglo males. The acknowledgment by State Education Departments of other social groups through policies is a first step toward allowing members of those groups to affirm themselves and their culture in the curriculum. Basal publishers' compliance with these policies is a cause for celebration. "Because if literature is a mirror that reflects human life, then all children who read or are read to need to see themselves reflected as part of humanity" (Bishop, 1992, p.37), and basals that are still used in a high percentage of American classrooms can bring that literature to all children.

Multicultural children's literature is most often defined as "literature by and about people who are members of groups considered to be outside the sociopolitical mainstream of the United States" (Bishop, 1992a, p.39). Although Bishop, other literature experts, and educators refer most frequently to people of color within white society when they consider multicultural children's literature, Klassen (1993) argues that a definition must also include concepts of "ethnicity, race, language, gender, religion, exceptionality, region, rationality and social class" (p.51). With this broader definition in mind, I examined basal series that are widely available (D.C. Heath, 1991 and Macmillan, 1989) and those recently published (Harcourt Brace Jovanovich, 1993 and Silver Burdett-Ginn, 1993) in order to see the types of multicultural children's literature included and the ways in which teacher's manuals suggested that such literature should be treated in American elementary school classes.

MULTICULTURAL LITERATURE IN BASALS: 1989–1991

The response to the call for multicultural children's literature in basal readers has taken a variety of forms. Melting pot tokenism is a disingenuous way to deal with multiculturalism. "Melting pot books ignore all differences except physical ones: skin color and other racially-related physical features" (Bishop, 1982, p.33). Consider the adaptation of a selection from *How to Eat Fried Worms* (Rockwell, 1933) in the 1991 D.C. Heath Series. Rockwell's text has been simplified and

New illustrations create the illusion that this mainstream story is a form of multicultural children's literature.

new illustrations create the illusion that this mainstream story is a form of multicultural children's literature. For example, three originally Anglo protagonists have been transformed into an African American, an Asian American, and an Anglo American. Their names have not changed (Alvermann, *et al.*, 1991b, pp.12–27). The original illustrations reflect the social conditions of the Depression era and the often desperate economic times. In the adaptation, not only has the authenticity of the literature been compromised, but the very social context of the story has been misrepresented. In this attempt to accommodate multicultural concerns the cultural foundation of the book has been changed.

Consider Harcourt Brace Jovanovich's adaptation of a selection from the chapter book . . . *and Now Miguel* (Krumgold, 1953), which presents a particular historical period within the conservative, religious, Spanish-speaking communities of northern New Mexico. The language and culture of these isolated communities still reflect the original seventeenth-century Spanish settlers. However, in the adaptation, culture seems sacrificed for reading experience. The focus of the basal selection is on one incidence in Miguel's life: the day he joins the sheep-shearing crew. On the verge of manhood, Miguel places great significance on this event. Much to his dismay, he falls into the bag of sheared wool and is rescued amidst the jovial jesting of the crew and family members. In the following quote from the original text, Miguel situates the full episode within a regional cultural context:

> I heard Johnny Marquez . "Sheep up!" That was him, his voice. For a second I thought to get mad at Johnny Marquez. But in the next second I thought not. Because there was not reason to be mad at Mr. Marquez. He had not given to me any promise. It was not him who said that he was arranging anything for San Ysidro. It was me, Miguel who figured

that out. My idea. All of it, everything was just something I decided in my own mind. About the miracle. And there wasn't any miracle. About San Ysidro hearing my wish. And San Ysidro he didn't hear anything, he didn't know I was alive, San Ysidro. About me becoming part of the whole crew. And all it was, I swept with the broom. About me being a new hand, with a new name, Twister. And all it was, a joke. About sitting down first with the men who ate first. A joke, too, that's all it was. (Krumgold, 1953, p.169)

The basal adaptation ends in the following manner:

I made myself small and I got up. I walked away from the shearing shed across the yard, without looking back. No one called me to look back, and there was no one I wanted to see. (Heald-Taylor, 1989c, p.186)

Even prayer doesn't escape the disingenuous treatment.

D.C. Heath published the following Kwakiutl poem beneath the title "Older But Wiser":

> What of olden times,
> shall I tell you of older times?
> What of olden times
> my grandchildren?
> (Alvermann, *et al.*, 1991c, p.321)

In the original, a Kwakiutl grandfather is telling stories to his grandchildren in the depths of winter (the culturally appropriate time for story telling in this Native American culture). However, the basal illustration depicts an African American grandfather and grandchild, seated upon the top of a hill on a lovely spring day. The child is flying a kite.

Chukka's Hawk, a story by Elizabeth Whitmore published by D.C. Heath, is an example of a transcultural selection (Alvermann, *et al.*, 1991b, pp.38–48), which

This attitude towards the desert, as empty space, contradicts reality and Native American beliefs.

Rudine Sims Bishop (1992b) defines as literature about one cultural group written by a member of another cultural group. Whitmore's Chukka, a contemporary Native American boy, is a member of a nameless generic Southwestern Indian tribe. This tribe appears to be an amalgam of Pueblo peoples, the Navajo, the Hopi, and perhaps the Tohono O'Ohdam and the Pima Indians of southern Arizona. Judging by the belt buckles and silver adornments that Chukka's uncle wears, one might assume the family to be Navajo, yet the traditional architecture is represented by a Pueblo-style dwelling with many large, decorated pieces of pottery visible in the foreground. Chukka's people herd sheep, and raise corn and beans on a land dotted with the mesas of the Four Corners area of northern Arizona. Proudly visible at the feet of these mesas are the Saguaro cacti of the great Arizona Sonoran Desert hundreds of miles to the south. It appears that the illustrations complement misinformation presented in the text. The men herd sheep, learn to use a bow and arrows, plant corn and beans, and weave, while the women appear to be restricted to child care and household duties. Women's roles are certainly misrepresented if this "tribe" is to be considered Navajo; the Navajo people are matrilineal, and women herd sheep and weave historically well-known Navajo blankets and rugs. Finally, Chukka speaks of the desert: ". . . when he was out in the desert, he did not feel big. He did not feel brave. The desert was hot and quiet and as empty as the sky" (Alvermann, *et al.*, 1991b, p.44). This attitude towards the desert, as empty space, contradicts reality and Native American beliefs about the significance of the land to their physical, cultural, and spiritual survival. Conspicuously absent in this modern story is the ever-present and necessary means of transportation on the vast reservations of the Southwest: the pickup truck.

These examples from two basals used in the Southwest and across the country demonstrate a lack of cultural sensitivity among basal publications. Often their attempts to include multicultural children's literature substitutes one culture or race for another as if they are indistinguishable and interchangeable. Although multicultural children's literature was included in these 1989 and 1991 editions, it does not seem to command much respect; the text is altered without reason, the illustrations serve to confuse, and the teacher's manuals do not make systematic or substantial attempts to develop cross-cultural understanding. I found it easy to doubt the multicultural sincerity of the authors, editors, and publishers of these series.

MULTICULTURAL CHILDREN'S LITERATURE IN BASALS: 1993

The use of multicultural children's literature in basal series seems to take a positive turn as I reviewed two 1993 series: Harcourt Brace Jovanovich's *Treasury of Literature* (Farr & Strickland, *et al.*, 1993), and Silver Burdett-Ginn's *New Dimensions in the World of Reading* (Baumann, *et al.*, 1993). Both contain specific statements on multiculturalism and multicultural children's literature by well-known educators, working in the field of multicultural education. Harcourt Brace Jovanovich has included two scholarly articles, one by Junko Yokota Lewis and Rolando R. Hinojosa-Smith, and the other by Asa G. Hilliard III. The 1993 Silver Burdett-Ginn series offers Carl Grant's three-stage cultural appreciation model.

Harcourt Brace Jovanovich—Treasury of Literature

In the philosophy statement at the beginning of the teacher's manual, multiculturalism is described as a central focus of this series. "Multicultural advisors helped to shape each phase of the program," (A. Hilliard III, Farr & Strickland, *et al.*, 1993e, p.R32). The Harcourt Brace Jovanovich *Treasury of Literature* offers a socially responsible reading curriculum by helping children in their quest for knowledge and truth" (Farr & Strickland, *et al.*, 1993e, p.432) and by providing cultural awareness notes, multicultural perspectives and multicultural connections. That is, multicultural children's literature is included to help children appreciate both the similarities and differences among differing cultures. Dr. Lewis and Dr. Hinojosa-Smith describe the criteria for selection of multicultural children's literature. The literature must: "1) be of literary and aesthetic merit, 2) provide a culturally conscious view of people and 3) facilitate a variety of cultural experiences" (Farr & Strickland, *et al.*, 1993, p.R30–R31). The "curriculum [is] based on the truth of the whole human experience" (Farr & Strickland, *et al.*, 1993, p.R32).

Using an expanded definition of multicultural literature as a guide, I looked at first-, third-, and fifth-grade levels of the Harcourt Brace Jovanovich series. The first- and third-grade anthologies seemed to include less multicultural children's literature than earlier series (1989–1991) I surveyed; however, the fifth-grade reader had a much more comprehensive selection of multicultural children's literature (close to 50 percent). Although the presence of the literature is significant, the treatment of that literature as part of the readers' responses to the literature must also be appraised.

For example, consider the contextual treatment of the cross-cultural Children's Choice Award (1987) picture book, *Jamaica's Find* by Juanita Havill, published in the first-grade anthology (Farr & Strickland, *et al.*, 199e, p.T301–309). Ms. Havill is an Anglo American; Jamaica is an African American child. In Rudine Sims Bishop's classification scheme, *Jamaica's Find* could be either a melting pot or transcultural text. The story line is quite simple. While playing in the park Jamaica finds a red hat and a stuffed dog. She turns the red hat in to the lost and found; she takes the cuddly stuffed dog home. The next day, after a conscience-ridden night, Jamaica takes the stuffed dog to the lost and found. Within a few minutes she meets Kristin, the Anglo American girl who lost the dog. Kristin and the dog are reunited. And the story ends as a friendship buds between the two girls.

However, the story in the first-grade reader doesn't end here. The publishers surround the story with lesson plans covering three main categories: Reading, responding, and learning through literature. I found *more than 50 lessons and activities* designed for use *before, during,* and *after* the reading of *Jamaica's Find.* Examples of these include vocabulary strategies, strategic reading (preview and predict, setting a purpose), guided reading, story follow ups, summarizing, literature appreciation, critical thinking activities, decoding (review of the long e and long a), study skills, test taking skills, comprehension strategies, and a writer's workshop. Included are activities and strategies that relate the story across the language arts, integrate the story across the curriculum, aid in meeting individual needs such as second-language support, and provide opportunities for cooperative learning and learning centers. It may be safe to say that any multicultural principles Havill had in mind are lost in the avalanche of skills and strategy lessons (Farr & Strickland, *et al.,* 1993, p.T296).

For instance, the multicultural perspectives lesson draws a connection between Jamaica's discovery of the right thing to do (return lost property) and an African American scientist, Lewis Howard Latimer's discovery of a way to make light bulbs last longer. The teacher is instructed to read aloud three paragraphs about Latimer. Children are then encouraged to make an award that is to be presented to "Latimer" during a role play. The teacher is also instructed to discuss with the children the ways in which lighting

It may be safe to say that any multicultural principles Havill had in mind are lost in the avalanche of skills and strategy lessons (Farr & Strickland, et al., 1993, p.T296).

has changed from early times to current times (Farr & Strickland, *et al.*, 1993, p.T326). I am at a loss to see the multicultural connection in these "discoveries." And I wonder if the author and the editors see the possible racist interpretation of teaching African Americans to return property that is not theirs.

Silver Burdett-Ginn—New Dimensions in the World of Reading

As I compared the 1993 update to its 1991 counterpart, I began to notice a significant change in the rhetoric surrounding and the treatment of multicultural children's literature. Carl Grant, a nationally known expert in multicultural education, seems to have been influential in very short time span. Although listed as an advisory author for the 1991 edition, Grant is an author for the 1993 teacher's edition. Grant includes race, gender, physical disability, and socio-economic class in his concept of multiculturalism (Baumann *et al.*, 1993c, p.T642) and presents his Cultural Appreciation Model: awareness and understanding, appreciation, and acceptance. These three concepts are woven throughout the teacher's editions with charts that identify the connections of specific reading selections and the three stages. Beyond Grant's stages, the teacher's manual offer three specific directions for teachers to conduct discussions of related issues among themselves. In addition, one-page information sheets offer very short paragraphs about multicultural education. Each sheet has numerous quotations related to issues of multicultural education around its border, quotations that provide a range of cultural and political perspectives from Edna Ferber to Henry Giroux (Baumann, *et al.*, 1993c, p.T642 & 760).

Silver Burdett-Ginn offers approximately 20 percent more multicultural children's literature in the anthologies than they did in 1991. While all together the multicultural children's literature exemplifies an expanded definition of multicultural education, it continues to rely most heavily on folktales and fiction from around the world, and the least amount of representation is given to American parallel cultures (Bishop, 1992). All the multicultural children's literature is embedded in lessons designed to teach children to read. For example, *Brother Eagle, Sister Sky,* a picture book by Susan Jeffers (Baumann, 1993c, p.T812–821), is a selection in the third-grade anthology. It is a fairly complete adaptation of Jeffers' original (but controversial) illustrations and her adaptation of Chief Seattle's words on Native American environmental ethic. The text, coming down through the ages, provides a strong and compelling message: to waste or destroy nature and its wonders is to destroy life itself (Jeffers, 1991, end page).

Lessons surrounding this story focus on three main categories: Engaging the Reader, Reading and Responding, and Supporting the Reader. There are *more than 35 lessons and activities* designed for use *before, during* and *after* the reading of this selection, which include: discussion of key concepts, vocabulary strategies, building background, appreciating cultures, setting a purpose for reading, building meaning, strategies for reading, highlighting literature, conventions of language, reader's response, comprehension check, writing to learn, language link (present-tense verbs), spelling link (vowels influenced by r), and practice of reading aloud with expression (Baumann, *et al.*, 1993b, p.T809). Also included are activities and strategies that meet individual needs: second-language learners, at-risk students, special education students, and gifted and talented students. Strategies for integrating the curriculum and incorporating the full spectrum of language arts are also presented. Cooperative learning activities are also included. Additional related readings are suggested.

In a section called Appreciating Culture, teachers

are told of the controversy that surrounds the illustration of this book (Slapin & Searle, 1987). Jeffers does not try to portray the Native Americans of the Northwest authentically. Instead, the artwork is based on the knowledge of a number of Native American cultures, whose cultures are integrated into the illustrations (Baumann, *et al.*, 1993b, p.T812). Without explicit reference to this controversy "students are encouraged to use the illustrations to determine how many different Native American groups are represented in the illustrations" (Baumann, *et al.*, 1993b, p.T821). Finally, students are invited to do research on Native Americans who lived in the Northwest when the first settlers arrived and discuss how they (the students) might have felt about the settlers if they had been Native American during the period of western expansion (Baumann, *et al.*, 1993b, p.T823). These seem to be genuine attempts to help students to understand life from another social group's perspective.

In the fifth-grade anthology, an adaptation of Jane Yolen's (1967) *The Emperor and the Kite* is offered. The plot revolves around the Princess Djeow Seow's struggle to release her father, the Emperor, from his prison tower. Djeow Seow, the youngest and tiniest of the Emperor's children, was often neglected. During her long hours of solitude, she had plenty of opportunity to play with her favorite toy, a kite. Each morning and evening, as she flew her kite, a monk passed by and loudly recited a prayer. One day the prayer provided the princess with the clue with which to aid her father in his escape from the prison tower: let him fly free on the kite.

The Emperor and the Kite is situated within the same curricular context as *Brother Eagle, Sister Sky*. Differences in the lessons reflect only grade level, content, and context within the larger basal unit. The Appreciating Cultures sections preceding the story provide only information as to the setting of the story, the main character, and the significance of the word emperor, *i.e.*, similar to king (Baumann, *et al.*, 1993c, p.22), serving only to prepare students to read this particular story, but not to learn about Chinese culture.

The Appreciating Cultures section that follows the text addresses Djeow Seow's character traits. Here the wonderful sensitivity to culture in *Brother Eagle, Sister Sky* seems to be missing. The teacher's manual suggests that the teacher facilitate a discussion of the possible connections of patience, perseverance, and loyalty to the reader's lives (Baumann, *et al.*, 1993c, p.27). These are not cultural issues. Moreover, the teacher's manual does not address the significance of the monk in relation to Djeow Seow's heroism. In fact, it is the monk who provided the solution to the Emperor's predicament. Djeow Seow is praised for her patience, perseverance, and loyalty to her father, but are these attributes that girls should have? Where is a historical probe of the treatment of women in China or the United States? Or is it the Chinese who need patience, perseverance, and loyalty?

Where is a historical probe of the treatment of women in China or the United States?

DOING MULTICULTURALISM IN BASAL READING SERIES

What has really happened to the multicultural children's literature and the issue of multiculturalism within the context of the 1993 basal reader? Although there are changes to be celebrated, multicultural children's literature is only a vehicle or instrument around which a multitude of diverse skills and strategies are taught, reviewed, and/or tested. These diverse skills and strategies speak to the eclecticism of basals reviewed here. Multiculturalism is but one strand, just a component, within the larger basal management system. It's more than the afterthought it used to be, but it's certainly not the focus of basal reading series.

What I find seriously lacking in basal treatment of multicultural children's literature is a perspective that goes beyond the selective tradition in children's literature.

In the process of reducing multiculturalism to another component the issue itself becomes clouded and somewhat suspect. For every genuine opportunity to learn about diverse cultures—the Appreciating Culture section of *Brother Eagle, Sister Sky*—there is a silly and often insulting attempt—Jamaica's and Latimer's "discoveries." Although race relations seem to be a priority in the selection of literature, basal publishers don't seem to know how to discuss or consider women or culture. Seldom does a teacher's manual ask teachers and students to use multicultural children's literature to explore themselves or other social groups in anything but superficial ways.

I find Grant's Cultural Appreciation Model in Silver Burdett-Ginn's basal limited. In fact, Grant and Christine Sleeter have set forth a much stronger model of education that is both multicultural and social reconstructivist (1989, p.46–65). This latter model suggests that literacy should help minority groups to name and struggle against their oppression and oppressors. This model prizes agency and activism—two elements absent from Harcourt Brace Jovanovich's and Silver Burdett-Ginn's treatment of multiculturalism. If basal publishers are serious about multiculturalism they owe it to teachers to explain why Grant's rhetoric has been domesticated in basal manuals. Perhaps, their treatment of multiculturalism is the clearest example of how basal publishers assimilate whatever they adopt to their stake in the status quo.

What I find seriously lacking in basal treatment of multicultural children's literature is a perspective that goes beyond the selective tradition in children's literature, *i.e.*, literature that exemplifies the dominant cultural ideology and does not address the issue of deferential power relations in our society (Christian-Smith, 1989; Taxel, 1981). The selective tradition can be countered by the oppositional texts (Taxel, 1981) that open the door to literature that reflects the multicultural web of our society, allows many voices to be heard, and explores the issue of differential power relations in our society (Taxel, 1981; Harris, 1986).

Moreover, basal reading series as examples of Western scientific thought are really contradictions to the concept of multiculturalism. Basals continue to represent linear, Western perceptions of ways of knowing, learning, and doing, while multiculturalism requires other voices and ways of knowing be validated. Without serious consideration of Eastern philosophy, women's ways of knowing, and native transcendentalism, basals provide a tourists' sweep through other cultures and ways of thinking and acting. This mismatch between theories about reading and multiculturalism cannot help students to better understand themselves and others. Rather, the attempt to assimilate the mismatch reduces the role of literacy in all cultures to a standard form that has been used for generations to systematically disadvantage disenfranchised groups. Basal series are at least partly responsible for this shameful history. In this sense, even with more multicultural children's literature and some well-intentioned exercises, a multicultural basal is truly an oxymoron. For example, the Civil Rights Era seems to end with the reflection of Rosa Parks. Where are the voices of Jesse Jackson, Cesar Chavez, Dolores Huerta, Leonard Peltier, Malcolm X, Gloria Steinem, Michael Harrington, San Day, Lois Gibs, and many others, all of which are available in children's and young adult literature?

7

NEITHER GONE NOR FORGOTTEN: TESTING IN NEW BASAL READERS[1]

SHARON MURPHY

The tests appeared to be built on a narrow and pseudoscientific approach to testing.

In *Report Card on Basal Readers* (Goodman, Shannon, Freeman, and Murphy, 1988), we argued that the testing component of the basal reader was the epitome of basal reader technology. With simplified texts that drew heavily on the principles of repetition and reinforcement, the basal reader tests echoed the principles of the basal reader programs themselves. Furthermore, the tests appeared to be built on a narrow and pseudoscientific approach to testing in that they contained many of the surface features of standardized tests that are not rigorous in terms of test design and do not reflect modern reading theory.

Since 1988, a new generation of basal reading pro-

[1] Funding for this research was provided by both a NCTE Research Foundation grant and a York University Faculty of Education Minor Research Award.

grams has entered the educational marketplace. Recently, I examined the testing programs of D.C. Heath Reading (Alvermann *et al.*, 1989/1991), the Harcourt Brace Jovanovich Reading Program Laureate Edition (1989a), Houghton Mifflin Literature Experience (1991), Scott Foresman Reading: An American Tradition (1989a), and Silver Burdett-Ginn World of Reading (1989/1990/1992) by taking every test at the first-, third-, and fifth-grade levels and reading all the information provided about assessment in the manuals.[2] What has changed? The short, but general answer is, not much of substance.

PLENTIFUL PURPOSES AND AN ADD-ON MENTALITY

New basal reading programs are replete with tests of many kinds, and now include even more types of assessment than were previously included. Added to or replacing placement tests, end-of-section tests, end-of-book tests, end-of-level tests, and skills tests are devices labeled theme tests, strategy assessment, holistic writing assessments, informal reading inventories, and attitude checklists. Although new devices have been added, they have not substantially reduced the amount of testing that students might experience. In 1988, if a first grader took all the tests possible for the basal reading program (excluding alternate forms), the range of items the student would compete was between 256 and 1578, depending on the program. The range for the new series is between 373 items (Houghton Mifflin) and 1086 (Scott Foresman). First graders complete up to three times as many

---

[2] The references to four of the programs are without authors' names because no authorship is assigned to the tests of those programs. Although the reference list contains the general name of the program, only the independent test/assessment components were examined.

items as fifth graders except in the case of Scott Foresman, in which the highest number of items is at the
third-grade level (1290) and the lowest is at the first-
grade level (1086).

Adding assessment formats to the already swollen
assessment programs in basals means that teachers
are swamped in a sea of theoretical eclecticism as to
what assessment should be. For example, Silver Burdett-Ginn touts one set of tests as an objectives-based
system and another set as a holistic informal assessment program.

> Unit Skills Tests. . . . are to help you manage instruc-
> tion. . . . they provide rich diagnostic information.
> Unit Process Tests. . . . measure general reading
> comprehension . . . and are holistic in their approach
> to reading assessment.
> End of Book Tests. . . . are general survey instru-
> ments which are to help you decide how well students
> have achieved the critical objectives of the entire level.
> The results . . . suggest a student's readiness to ad-
> vance.
> Mid-Book Tests. . . . provide a cumulative as-
> sessment.
> Placement Tests. . . . for determining initial level as-
> signment.
> Informal Reading Inventory. . . . provides an alterna-
> tive method of placing students. (Silver Burdett-Ginn,
> 1992, Informal Reading Inventory, p.1).

Publishers appear to be struggling to keep up with the latest trends and the buzz words in assessment and literacy education.

Publishers appear to be struggling to keep up with
the latest trends and the buzz words in assessment
and literacy education, while they maintain the assessment features of the past. For instance, Heath and
Silver Burdett-Ginn provide guides to portfolio assessment. Both guides portray the types of information necessary to document reading as a multifaceted
and complex process. Silver Burdett-Ginn's guide is
somewhat more open-ended than Heath's. However,
neither publisher discusses how to fit basal tests
within their articulated principles for portfolio assess-

ment such as "risk-taking and experimentation should be celebrated." Given the history behind basal tests in school districts, efforts to expand classroom assessment of reading must begin with such discussions.

THEORETICAL EMPHASIS WITHIN THE TESTS

In 1988, the emphasis in first-grade testing programs was on word identification and word parts. This emphasis gradually decreased across the grades, which mirrored the instructional programs. Little has changed in most of the new programs. Six item types were clear while I took the basal tests: nonword (which did not focus on print), subword (which looked at word parts), word (which did not provide syntactic or semantic cues), phrasal (which were sentence fragments), sentence (which were one or two sentences in length), and discourse (which involved texts of more than two sentences in length). With the exception of Harcourt Brace Jovanovich, the pattern of decreasing emphasis on word or subword items across grades continues. First-grade programs ranged between 49.5 percent (Heath) and 71.5% (Harcourt Brace Jovanovich) for word or subword items. By third grade this emphasis among items decreased to between 0% (Silver Burdett-Ginn) and 18.4% (Heath), and from 0% (Silver Burdett-Ginn) to 12.6% (Heath) for the fifth-grade tests.

A decreasing emphasis on words did not necessarily mean an increase in the amount of discourse items that students experience in basal tests. For instance, over half of the items on the Scott Foresman and Harcourt Brace Jovanovich fifth-grade tests focused on phrasal or sentence items. Discourse items ranged from 9.9% (Scott Foresman) to 40.8% (Houghton Mifflin) of first-grade tests; 33.3% (Scott Foresman) to 59.2% (Silver Burdett-Ginn) for third-grade tests; and 33% (Harcourt Brace Jovanovich) to 73.6% (Houghton

Mifflin) for fifth-grade tests. Some publishers have a
long way to go in order to develop tests that parallel
everyday reading tasks.

LENGTH OF TEXTS WITHIN TESTS

In 1988, the length of texts used in tests ranged from
6 to 164 words for first grade, from 35 to 574 words
for third grade, and 70 to 701 words for fifth grade. As
Table 1 illustrates, most new basals have maintained a

Program	Average Words Per Text	Maximum Average Words Per Text in Each Subtest	Minimum Average Words Per Text in Each Subtest
D. C. Heath			
Gr. 1	58.0	157.5	11.2
Gr. 3	197.1	448.9	89.6
Gr. 5	242.3	360.0	89.8
HBJ			
Gr. 1	66.0	582.0	14.0
Gr. 3	184.9	1109.0	57.0
Gr. 5	244.5	486.0	130.1
Houghton Mifflin			
Gr. 1	272.9	1454.0	56.0
Gr. 3	457.1	2485.0	80.0
Gr. 5	706.1	2625.0	50.0
Scott Foresman			
Gr. 1	20.3	41.5	11.8
Gr. 3	125.1	214.3	52.0
Gr. 5	160.7	329.7	32.8
Silver Burdett-Ginn			
Gr. 1	114.0	259.5	27.7
Gr. 3	291.0	546.3	69.0
Gr. 5	470.0	852.0	223.0

Table 1   Average Length of Texts in Basal Reading Tests

comparable length with only Houghton Mifflin using substantially longer texts than before. In their theme tests, Houghton Mifflin includes multiple texts on one particular topic in an attempt to create a theme environment, thus increasing the amounts of text upon which items are based.

QUALITY OF TEST ITEMS

It is important to analyze basal tests for their compliance with test theory as well as their textual focus. Such analyses are ultimately aimed at the validity of the tests themselves, because if test items do not appear to assess the areas for which they were intended, then it is problematic to make inferences about students' reading abilities based on their performances on these tests. Although the list of problems differs from the one I generated in 1988, basal test items are not always "good items." One major improvement has been the elimination of the multiple choice formats for letter identification of the first-grade tests in which the item distracters were labeled with letters of the alphabet.

Because of their emphasis on word analyses, first-grade tests rely heavily on illustrations. Unfortunately, each test includes problematic illustrations, including drawings that could not readily be identified unless someone named them, two different names for the same illustration within a single subtest, and ambiguities caused when actions are depicted or when part of an object is the focus of the item rather than the whole object. For Heath and Houghton Mifflin, less than one percent of the illustrations had such problems, but the Silver Burdett-Ginn, approximately ten percent of the items had problems with the illustrations. There are no problems with the illustrations included in any third- or fifth-grade tests.

Because basal tests are criterion-referenced, they

are targeted towards the mastery of specific skills. In order to identify whether or not a skill has been mastered, both the correct response and the distracters must be generated in a way that tightly reflects the skill that is being assessed. For example, if the skill is the long sound of "a" in one-syllable words, then distracters should be one syllable words with a short "a" sound or ones with another long vowel sound (*e.g.,* bike). If not all the items in a subtest follow this format, then additional skills are being assessed during the same subtest. As a consequence, a student's score on the subtest might not reflect his or her success or failure to master the targeted skill, rather the score could be influenced by the new information introduced through the inconsistency of item writing.

Every program I examined contained inconsistent patterns for generating items within subtests.

Every program I examined contained inconsistent patterns for generating items within subtests. This problem occurred at all grade levels for all basal tests with the exception of the Houghton Mifflin third- and fifth-grade tests and Heath fifth-grade tests. Inconsistent item writing occurred most often on first-grade tests (ranging from 6.62 percent for Heath to 45.4 percent for Harcourt Brace Jovanovich). The prevalence of these problems suggests that the deceptively simple word and subword tasks of first grade are more complex than the test writers and basal publishers seem to believe. Of course, inconsistency with subtests that effect the interpretation of subtest scores also makes the aggregate test scores suspect.

In 1988, we reported that many of the items that were intended to test the use of contextual support did not actually use tests that gave contextual support. When I looked at the new tests, I found that the basal publishers decided to make context their "cause celebre." In fact, they have placed context in many subtests where it serves no function at all. In the following example, the context does little to help a test taker eliminate distracters. For all intents and purposes, the item tests word identification.

[Task: The student is to find the opposite.]
Nick *closed* the door.
(a) took   (b) made   (c) opened
(Silver Burdett-Ginn, Make a Wish, Unit Test, Unit 2,
Item 11)

Nonfunctioning context was found at all levels of basal tests, except Heath and Harcourt Brace Jovanovich third-grade tests and Harcourt Brace Jovanovich, Houghton Mifflin, and Silver Burdett-Ginn fifth-grade tests. Twenty percent of Houghton Mifflin's third-grade items suffered from this problem.

When test developers create distracters for multiple choice tests, one distracter is supposed to be close to correct but demonstrably wrong. However, on all but the Houghton Mifflin tests, items included two plausible answers. For example, for the following item conceivably either *b* or *c* could be correct.

A big b__ld__r was stuck in the dirt near the road.
(a) rock   (b) builder   (c) boulder
(Scott Foresman, On Parade, Section Tests 3/2, Section 1, Item 13).

Sometimes there are no correct answers for readers to choose. For example, in one passage Ralph and Philip look unsuccessfully for a newspaper to find out about current movies. They then ask their siblings, who recommend several that they have seen. The two boys discuss their options and decide to attend a particular movie.

Ralph and Philip finally choose the movie they want to see by
(a)   consulting a newspaper
(b)   asking their brother
(c)   calling a friend
(d)   asking their sister
(Heath, Rare as Hen's Teeth, Unit Test 5, Item 21)

Option (b) is identified as correct, but the text clearly indicates that the boys made their choice through discussion. Although these problems occurred only about one percent of the time, they highlight the fact that readers are not being judged fairly, even when they do the right things.

In 1988, we reported that passage dependency of items was a problem with the basal tests that were reviewed. In other words, some questions could be answered without reading a passage. The new tests also have this problem. The lowest incidence was 2.6 percent of the items for Heath's first-grade test. The highest was Silver Burdett-Ginn's fifth-grade test, with 48.2 percent of the items; students could answer *half* of the questions without reading any text!

Lack of independence among items was another pattern observed in the new basal tests. Lack of independence means that two or more items are interconnected because either the question or answer of one item provides clues or is dependent on the answer of another item. This is problematic because each item is supposed to stand by itself. Not only does lack of independence among items decrease the validity and reliability of subtests by reducing the true number of items on a particular subtest, but it places test takers in double jeopardy. I found that all basal publishers had items that lacked independence. Scott Foresman had the lowest number (0 percent) on their first-grade test, and Silver Burdett-Ginn had the highest (10 percent) on their fifth-grade test.

New basal tests continue to exhibit problems with language. Item language is not cohesive, is incoherent, and at times, is inconclusive. A common example deals with past tense and direct address. A first-grade student would have to be familiar with complex punctuation to eliminate distracter (c) in the following item.

Kim _____ Meg find the box.
(a) helping   (b) helped   (c) help
(Harcourt Brace Jovanovich, New Friends, End of Book Test, Item 63)

*Publishers'
attempts to
include extracts
from children's
literature in their
tests causes
problems with
unconnected or
ambiguous
referents.*

Ironically, publishers' attempts to include extracts from children's literature in their tests causes problems with unconnected or ambiguous referents.

NOTEWORTHY DEVELOPMENTS

Although their number is limited, there are some improvements in the assessment programs of the new basals. At this point they are merely add-ons, but they are improvements nonetheless. First, Houghton Mifflin presents text on their theme tests in a graphic environment similar to that which students encounter in the basal readers themselves. In other words, they include interesting illustrations in formats not necessarily designed to maximize space on a page. This correspondence makes the test more like school reading.

Houghton Mifflin and Heath have included open-ended responses along with multiple choice formats. For at least some of the items in these formats, the questions demand complex answers rather than the reproductive and narrow responses of most multiple choice items. However, Houghton Mifflin has begun to experiment with multiple answer multiple choice formats, increasing the likelihood of complex questions in multiple choice formats as well. Harcourt Brace Jovanovich has added holistic writing assessment, but it is woefully underdeveloped in its current format.

Finally, I have somewhat mixed reactions to several companies' use of children's literature and other authentic texts in their tests. Granted these texts are improvements on the impoverished texts of old, but because the items and philosophy of the tests have not been improved, I worry that tests with children's literature may lead children away from the love of literature that the publishers say they are trying to foster in the rest of their program. Certainly, the authors of these children's books did not write them with reading assessment in mind, and children rarely engage children's literature to test their abilities.

Tests are neither gone nor forgotten in the new basal series in the United States. Many of the problems we found in 1988 persist. Publishers have added more ways to measure what they define as reading instead of doing something substantive to change their basic approach to assessment. Although publishers' early cosmetic changes in basal tests may be signposts toward more substantial changes in the future, right now publishers are not seriously engaged in the challenge to create authentic assessment for literacy experiences. That is, basal publishers have yet to confront modern literacy theory or cutting edge views of assessment. Rather, they continue to produce tests based on ideas that are being rejected by cognitive psychologists (*e.g.*, Resnick and Resnick, 1990), reading theorists (*e.g.*, Goodman, 1982; Valencia and Pearson, 1987) and teachers (Harman, 1991). It is time for basal publishers to assess their own views on assessment. They are failing their own tests.

8

CELEBREMOS LA LITERATURA: IS IT POSSIBLE WITH A SPANISH READING PROGRAM?

YVONNE S. FREEMAN

In the 1990 census, 17.4 million people in the United States reported that they spoke Spanish at home (Barringer, 1993).

Celebremos la Literatura (Let's Celebrate Literature) and *Estrellas de la Literatura* (Stars of Literature) are the titles of two 1993 literature-based Spanish language reading programs. Both *Celebremos la Literatura* (Houghton Mifflin) and *Estrellas de la Literatura* (Harcourt Brace Jovanovich) include a wide range of quality Spanish language literature in their programs. The promotional materials of both programs emphasize this literature and its centrality to the teaching of reading. But can these basal programs really, as the Houghton Mifflin title suggests, celebrate reading?

This question is as important for Spanish language basal programs as it is for English language programs. A tremendous market has developed for educational materials in Spanish. In the 1990 census, 17.4 million people in the United States reported that they spoke Spanish at home (Barringer, 1993). Large numbers of children are Spanish speaking when they enter school. In California alone over one million students in grades K-12 were identified as second language learners in 1992. Of those, 862,036 spoke Spanish as their first language (California, 1992).

With so many Spanish-speaking students in our schools, publishers have responded by producing Spanish language materials. Until recently, teachers were so desperate that they welcomed any books in Spanish, no matter what the quality. However, now that many Spanish language books and other materials of excellent quality are available, it is critical that educators understand that using literature simply because it is printed in Spanish does not necessarily help Spanish/English bilingual teachers or students. In other words, bilingual educators can afford to be choosy when deciding what books to use to teach Spanish reading.

SPANISH LANGUAGE BASAL READERS

In 1987, I did a thorough review of the six Spanish-language basal reading programs in the United States (Freeman, 1987, 1988a, 1988b, 1988c). They were:

Hagamos Caminos (1986) Addison Wesley
Economy Spanish Reading Series (1987) Economy
Programa de Lectura en Español (1986)
Mil maravillas (1986) Macmillan
Reading in Two Languages (1984) Santillana
Focus: Leer para Triunfar (1986) Scott Foresman

The purpose of that study was to determine whether the basal materials published to teach Spanish reading reflect what research has shown about the reading process (Freeman, 1987). The conclusions were reached by looking at 170 characteristics of the materials using The Spanish Program Profile Instrument, an adaptation of an instrument developed by

Goodman and Page (1978). Since these programs are still widely used, I will offer briefly my conclusions about those basals before presenting an analysis of the 1993 editions. Although no two programs studied were exactly alike, the six programs studied were more the same than they were different. In fact, in 1987, Scott Foresman's *Spanish Reading* and Macmillian's *Capanitas de Oro* (Little Golden Bells) were published without significant differences from the six basals I originally studied.

Most of what students read, except for the poetry, has been adapted or translated from English.

The 1980s materials teach reading through syllabic, word, or use of cueing systems approaches, but the ultimate goal of the many skill exercises is word identification. The promotional materials and the teacher's guides stress the importance of context for comprehensions, but the exercises reflect a very limited view of context. In many stories and exercises, context consists of a single sentence. Further, questions, exercises, and tests reflect the view that reading is a product to be measured rather than a process to be experienced. In Spanish basals, reading is approached by having students master skills in a step-by-step, part-to-whole manner.

According to these lessons, language is habit. Students using the materials are given simplified, repetitious text and questions that call for stimulus-response kinds of interactions. Skill and vocabulary exercises, organized by an elaborate scope and sequence, are intended to help students achieve mastery of reading by following a carefully controlled step-by-step procedure. Although several publishers advertise their series as containing an excellent selection of Spanish literature, most of what students read, except for the poetry, has been adapted or translated from English even at the advanced levels. The materials do not provide the resources that allow students to experience the richness of the Spanish language through authentic Spanish literature.

The materials in the six programs dictate what

learners do and when and how they should do it. The basal materials often drive the curriculum. Learners are viewed as passive and dependent. Basal authors hold the assumption that the materials themselves contain everything necessary for students to learn to read. Because of this assumption, the teachers using basal programs are seen as technicians following directions rather than as professionals making decisions.

The first lines of a text in one of the preprimers help illustrate some of the above conclusions.

> *Toditos Saltan* (Everyone Jumps)
> Son sapitos y saltan solitos. (They are little frogs and they jump all by themselves.) Son ositos y saltan solitos. (They are little bears and they jump all by themselves.) Son patitos y saltan solitos. (They are little ducks and they jump all by themselves.) (*Lluvias Cantantes*, p.13, student text of *Economy Spanish Reading Series* 1987).

Vocabulary is carefully controlled to reflect recoding skill practice exercises of syllables with the vowels /a/, /i/, and /o/ and the consonants /s/, /p/, /t/, /ll/, and /n/. The surrounding context is so limited that pictures alone provide clues to meaning. In this case, all the animals in the picture accompanying the text, including the frogs, are on pogo sticks to show the young reader that all the animals are jumping. (It might be noted, however, that many children might not recognize a pogo stick or know its function.) In texts such as this one, learners passively recite repetitious lines. Teachers are to lead students through stilted readings that are not really stories at all because the texts themselves carry little meaning, and then, to direct students through a lengthy set of exercises to teach those syllables, vowels, and consonant sounds.

RECENT SPANISH BASAL PROGRAMS

Since my 1987 study a great deal of attention has been given to children's literature in Spanish. Publishers have expanded the limited and flawed resources available five years ago. Now bookstores and distributors from around the world have specialized in literature and other materials in Spanish, and different agencies have compiled bibliographies of new Spanish materials (for sources consult California State Department of Education, 1991; Freeman & Freeman, 1992; Freeman & Cervantes, 1991; Freeman & Cervantes, 1993; Schon, 1992). Drawing on the authentic, quality literature available, Harcourt Brace Jovanovich and Houghton Mifflin produced new programs for bilingual teachers and students in 1993. Harcourt Brace Jovanovich's *Estrellas de la Literatura* expresses a desire to meet the literature needs of bilingual classrooms by opening each *guía del maestro* (teacher's manual) with a letter to the teacher describing the program:

> *HBJ Estrellas de la Literatura* is an integrated reading and language arts program that uses literature to support and enhance Spanish-speakers' oral and written literacy . . . *HBJ Estrellas de la Literatura* offers your students a collection of authentic literature to instill pride in their cultural heritage. The award-winning selections range from classics to contemporary fiction and nonfiction from Spain, Mexico, and other Latin American countries. By nurturing a lifelong love of reading and language, the program sets the foundation for bilingual literacy.

In one of their promotional brochures, Houghton Mifflin describes its *Programa de Lectura: ¡Celebremos la Literatura!*:

> Once upon a time . . . Houghton Mifflin brought together a unique group of Hispanic writers, combined their creativity with literature from other Spanish-

This does not mean that basal publishers celebrate the literature that they include in the anthologies.

speaking cultures, and added the literature-based instructional system of the successful *Houghton Mifflin Reading: The Literature Experience.* The result: the most exciting Spanish reading program ever created is now available for your classroom!

Both programs do indeed provide literature in Spanish that is appropriate for students in the United States. Although there is still a great need for more literature about the Mexican American experience written by Mexican American authors (Barrera, Liguori, & Salas, 1992), Houghton Mifflin's *Celebremos* series sought out Hispanic authors in the United States to write stories and poetry about Hispanic children in the United States. Both series include a wide variety of Spanish children's literature and include photographs and art work in introductory sections throughout the books that reflect the students who will be reading the stories. This is a dramatic step in the right direction, and other companies are following suit. In preparation for a new literature-based program, Scott Foresman has asked bilingual teachers in several school districts to provide lists of the literature books in Spanish that the teachers think are good for their bilingual students. The new literature is a cause for celebration. However, this does not mean that basal publishers celebrate the literature that they include in the anthologies. Because publishers continue to package the Spanish children's literature within lessons designed to teach words and skills, they offer teachers and students literature-based programs rather than literature on which teachers can base their programs.

LITERATURE-BASED PROGRAMS VERSUS LITERATURE PROGRAMS

One way to examine literature-based programs is to compare them with programs that use authentic literature (Freeman, 1989, 1991; Freeman & Goodman, in press). Table 1 summarizes the comparison.

Assumptions

Literature-Based   *vs.*   *Literature*

Literature-based Reading	Literature Reading
Literature can be sequenced into grade levels.	Literature is universal across ages
All students at certain levels should read the same books.	Students at all levels should choose what they read.
All students will get the same meaning from a piece of literature.	Readers get different meanings from a piece of literature.
All students at each grade level have the same interests and backgrounds.	Students have varied interests and backgrounds.
Literature is embodied in books, mostly stories.	Literature is embodied in a wide range of language genres.

Literature-based Learners	Literature Learners
Have no real choices	Have choice
Controlled by the materials	Control the materials
Find someone else's meaning	Construct meaning for themselves
Answer someone else's questions	Answer their own questions
Write what is suggested	Write their own responses to literature
Follow directions	Make decisions

Literature-based Teachers	Literature Teachers
Follow the lead of the materials	Follow the lead of the students
Are told what to teach and when	Decide with the students what they want to do and when
Use prepared instructional materials (workbooks, company prepared journals or units, comprehension questions)	Use materials written by professional authors and illustrators; materials students produce (participate in literature studies, write books, become experts on topics of interest)

Literature-based Materials	Literature Materials
Real, adapted, or unadapted literature	Real, unadapted literature
Anthologies	Unabridged literature
From textbook companies and other professional education materials publishers: workbooks, units, activity guides, summaries, comprehension questions	Bookstores, classrooms, schools and public libraries become the focal point for materials selections; students write their own materials

Table 1   Literature-Based Versus Literature

Although basal literature-based programs use real, quality literature, they require students to read certain books at certain grades or during certain parts of the program because the books are part of a program. *HBJ Estrellas de la Literatura* has six anthologies of literature for grade 1, three for grade 2, three for grade 3, and one each for grades 4 and 5. The series also has related big books with cassettes for the first three levels. Anthologies that organize stories around themes are designed to be used in the order presented. Houghton Mifflin's *Programa de Lectura: Celebremos la Literatura* calls for more flexibility because, as their teacher's manual explains, "At Houghton Mifflin, we recognize that instructional needs differ according to age and grade level" (p.14). However, pages 14 and 15 of the teacher's manual lays out which books and other materials the company has provided for each grade level, and teacher's manuals are organized following the suggested order. In literature programs, on the other hand, students and teachers select books and other materials that support their individual and class needs and interests.

The 1993 basal programs are free of the long lists of comprehension questions found in earlier programs where often there were "almost as many questions in the comprehension check-up as sentences in the story" (Goodman, *et al.*, 1988, p.79) and where "questions in basals tended to require single correct answers directly from the text" (p.81). However, the way the teacher's manual leads students and teachers through the stories limits opportunity for any individual construction of meaning. For example, in the teacher's guide for *Siempre Soñaba* (Always Dreaming), the last Level 1, Grade 1 anthology of *Celebremos la Literatura*, students are invited to read the story *Torta de Cumpleaños* (Birthday Cake) by Ivar Da Coll. The teacher's manual has the students read the first time "to find out what problem the animal characters have and how they resolve it" (p.23). Then the teacher is told exactly what to say for a "Think Aloud" with the children to help them "consider what a reader could do if he or she didn't understand why Horacio packed fruit in a basket":

> There is something I don't understand: why did Horacio pack fruit in a basket? Is he planning a picnic? What does that have to do with Ursula's birthday? Should I stop reading and give up because I don't understand this part of the story? I know that rereading sometimes helps me understand something so I'll try that. And then maybe if I read on a bit, the story will start to make some sense. (Read aloud pages 15–17.) Now I see what Horacio is up to. The fruit is a present for Ursula! No wonder I didn't understand; I never got fruit as a present. I didn't think of fruit as a present (p.23).

The comprehension questions have simply been replaced by scripted strategies such as this "Think Aloud."

In essence, the comprehension questions have simply been replaced by scripted strategies such as this "Think Aloud.". In contrast to this guided questioning, students and teachers in literature classrooms explore content and literature by engaging in investigations and literature studies together.

Control in the literature-based programs resides in the materials rather than in the learners or teachers. Like *Celebremos la Literatura*, *HBJ Estrellas de la Literatura* avoids traditional comprehension questions and makes an effort to have students build on their own background and interests by having them predict, set their own purposes, and respond to literature. However, again because the materials are sequenced and include step-by-step suggestions for teachers that all the students are to follow, it is difficult for students or teachers to really make their own decisions, answer their own questions, or create their own responses.

For example, in the *HBJ Estrellas* "Diari del Estudiante" (Student Diary) for Grado Cinco (Fifth Grade), *Lejos y Cerca* (Far and Near), six pages are provided for students to fill out in response to the story *Salven mi Selva* by Monica Zak. However, those six pages are really not a personal student response to the story but a series of six exercises that accompany six extra support readings written by company authors. Each reading also has a different activity page including the following: an exercise on synonyms, a page of short answer questions, a problem-solving activity, a summary paragraph to write, a page to write about an endangered animal of the student's choice, and a question to answer in response to a poem. Attempts are made to allow students to be creative in their responses. Questions are open-ended and topics included are of probable interest to many students. However, the "Diario" is really not a personal student diary at all, but a kind of workbook in disguise. When a classroom is a literature classroom, the control of the materials is in the hands of the students and teacher who construct their own meanings as they answer their own questions and create their own responses to literature.

In both *HBJ Estrellas de la Literatura* and in Houghton Mifflin's *Programa de Lectura: Celebremos la Literatura,* teacher's manuals lead teachers step-by-step through detailed lessons. For example, in *Alas y Olas* (Wings and Waves), the first grade 3 anthology of *HBJ Estrellas,* there are 32 pages in the teacher's manual for teaching the first story, *La Pequeña Wu-Li* (The Small Wu-Li) by Ricardo Alcántara. The teacher's manual outlines activities under general headings of reading the literature, rereading the literature, learning through literature, integrating the curriculum, and writer's workshop.

In Houghton Mifflin's Level 1 anthology, *Un Pequeño Ruido* (A Small Noise), the story, *Tacho: El Bebé Tacuache* (Tacho: The Baby Opossum) by Carmen Tafolla, is accompanied by 31 pages of teacher's manual support organized around what the teacher's manual authors describe as "shared reading" sections. There are, in fact, four types of shared reading activities for each story: Shared Reading 1: Reading for Interest; Shared Reading 2: Rereading for Comprehension; Shared Reading 3: Rereading for Language Patterns; and Shared Reading 4: Rereading for Decoding. While these different types of shared reading might be done in a literature classroom, the many activities suggested contradict the philosophy of shared reading. Manning and Fennancy (1993) explain what they hope teachers will understand about shared reading: "we do not teach children to read, but we can make it possible for them to teach themselves through texts that engage them" (p. 48). When teachers follow plans offered by the teacher's manual in reading programs, they are not allowing children "to teach themselves through texts that engage them." However, when teachers in literature classrooms use authentic texts including literature, magazines, newspapers, and student publications, they can follow the lead of their students and decide with their students what they want to do and when.

When teachers in literature classrooms use authentic texts including literature, magazines, newspapers, and student publications, they can follow the lead of their students.

Both *HBJ Estrellas de la Literatura* and Houghton Mifflin's *Programa de Lectura: Celebremos la Literatura* include a wide variety of unadapted and unabridged children's literature in Spanish. In addition, both programs offer literature apart from the anthology. A comparison of twenty stories in the anthologies of the two series with the original books revealed that neither the texts nor the illustrations in the original literature had been compromised in any way. In fact, in some cases, as in Leo Lionni's Spanish translation of *Tillie and the Wall* (*HBJ Estrellas de la Literatura*) the illustrations are larger than in the original book publications. The only difference found in *Tillie and the Wall* and some other books is that the print in the anthologies has been made somewhat larger and more blocked, like the print of beginning texts in past basal reading programs.

Translations of the literature into Spanish, a concern in some of the Spanish-language basal programs in the earlier study (Freeman, 1987), are not a problem in either program. Several translations in *HBJ Estrellas de la Literatura* and *Celebremos la Literatura* were critiqued by Jesús Serra, a well-known Venezuelan poet, and his wife, Marisela, a professor of reading in Venezuela. Both found the stories to be translated into clear, readable Spanish. It should also be added that a delightful feature of both series is the highlighting of the book authors and illustrators for the different stories.

The problem with the programs as we look at literature-based versus literature materials is, as mentioned earlier, the fact that both *Estrellas* and *Celebremos* are *programs*. While both programs set prices that allow schools to purchase the individual books and book sets separately, the teacher's manual lessons refer to the other available support materials. This creates the impression that these materials are necessary for using the literature. *Celebremos* offers big books, student anthologies, individually bound books, diaries, journal books, family resources, theme book plans, resource masters for duplication, instruction charts, instruction masters, family/home activity booklets, evaluation booklets, informal reading inventories, audiotapes, syllable, word, and picture cards, Texas evaluation booklets, and Texas Assessment blackline masters. *Estrellas* offers student anthologies, big books, literature cassettes, diaries, English as a second language manuals and posters, assessment guides including portfolio guides, and reading inventories. This partial listing of materials that accompany the literature-based programs helps us begin to understand that any *program* diverts teachers and students from the experience of reading wonderful books. When teachers provide real, unadapted and unabridged reading materials along with opportunities for choice and exploration, they can capture students' interest, challenge them to explore new avenues, and encourage them to read for pleasure.

CONCLUSION

Teachers must protect readers from some experiences so that they will continue to value reading. For example, *Julieta y su Caja de Colores,* written and illustrated by Carlos Pellicer López, is a beautifully told and illustrated story of Julieta, a young girl who is given a box of paints. She discovers how she can express herself, her feelings, and her world through painting. The story ends with the line "Saber pintar es saber decir las cosas" (To know how to paint is to know how to express yourself). One of the activity pages in the *Planes para la Lectura Individual* (Plans for Individual Reading) book (Houghton Mifflin, 1993 p. 2) for this story is a page with seven circles that contain the words that describe the things Julieta drew. Students are told to color the circles. Not only is the question factually incorrect (the whole point of the story was that Julieta had a set of paints and painted things–she didn't draw), but the coloring exercise to identify words trivializes the story and in a sense insults the author and the reader. This kind of disguised worksheet causes real concern for anyone attempting to help students respond to authentic literature.

In discussion with well-informed and well-meaning publisher consultants, there is a recurrent response when I object to the support materials that distort not only the literature, but the whole reading process. They explain that it is teachers and administrators that insist on these materials and that programs with less support materials do not make as much money as those with carefully sequenced programs. Whose responsibility is it to make these changes? My answer is that it is everyone's responsibility. Educators have the responsibility to demand only what is good for children. Publishers have a responsibility to produce only what they know from theory and research is appropriate.

I challenge basal publishers to continue to move

The literature in the 1993 Spanish language basal programs is reduced to coloring circles.

in a positive direction, to continue to publish quality literature, but to resist the temptation of making money through meaningless exercise. Since publishers understand the need for literature and authentic literature response but need a profit each year, they should offer students in schools choices of a variety of paperback books to use as they read, research, discuss, and do literature studies. Schools would then encourage the students to consider the books theirs to be taken home when they have read and responded to them. Each year these books would need to be replaced, and new and different books could also be purchased for students. This practice would fill homes with books, and publishers would make profits without promoting materials that do not support reading. To continue present practices means that the literature in the 1993 Spanish language basal programs is reduced to coloring circles. We can do better than this.

9

THE DESTINATION OR THE FIRST STEP ON A JOURNEY: CANADIAN BASALS

SHARON MURPHY

One sign of progress noted in the *Report Card on Basal Readers* (Goodman, Shannon, Freeman & Murphy, 1988) was recent developments in Canadian basals. We inferred this progress by briefly examining the philosophy statement of one Canadian program (Holt *Impressions*), and we lauded some of the components that appeared to distinguish Canadian basals from basals in the United States. Canadian basals offered big books, audiotapes to accompany students' independent reading, a writing program integrated with the reading program, and poetry anthologies for teachers to read to students. At the time, these features were a marked departure from the basals used in the United States.

Since then, I've looked beyond the "things" of the Canadian basals to their content and substance (Murphy, 1991, 1992). I examined Holt *Impressions* (Booth,

*Only one
publisher has
made changes in
its core program
since my initial
investigation.*

1984, 1985, 1987/1988), Ginn *Journeys* (Doyle, 1984), Nelson *Network* (McInnes, 1986/1987/1988; McInnes, Garry, Hearn & Hughes, 1983); McGraw-Hill *Unicorn* (Rennick, Armstrong, Deeth & Sutherland, 1984d), and Gage *Expressways II* (Thorn & Irwin, 1986/1987). Although the publication dates on these basals may seem old to teachers in the United States, only one publisher has made changes in its core program since my initial investigation.

Having just finished the *Report Card on Basal Readers* when I began this review, I was initially astonished by what I saw in the Canadian basals. At a surface level, they seemed miles ahead of United States basals. Furthermore, I was surprised to find that these basals were in print well before we undertook what we thought at the time was cutting edge critique of reading textbooks. To a large degree, however, my initial enthusiasm waned as I began to probe deeply into the Canadian programs.

THEMES CHARACTERIZING CANADIAN BASALS

The recent spate of new and improved "literature-based" or "whole language" basals in the United States (Flood, 1990; Perkins, 1989) echo the promises made by Canadian basals of the 1980s. Canadian basals are diversified. For instance, the Gage first-grade program contains one big book, four student anthologies, three student workalongs, three student theme activity books, three teacher source books, three mini-books, and three reading corners (with nine to eleven books per corner). This diversity does not decrease across grade levels. Fifth-grade Nelson contains two student anthologies, two student workbooks, one teacher's resource book, two novels, one teacher's handbook for novels, one evaluation resource guide, one reading and how, one writing and how, and two audiotapes. Traditional names for components have been changed. Gone is the "basal reader;" here is the "student anthology." Gone is "teacher's manual;" here is the "source book" or "resource book." In most cases, this diversity and these changes were more cosmetic than a fundamental switch in underlying assumptions. Let me be explicit.

Goodbye Dick and Jane?

At the first-grade level, Canadian basals rely heavily on patterned text. When the term "patterned text" was first used in the early 1980s, it was grounded in discussion of predictable books (Bridge, Winograd, & Haley, 1983; Heald-Taylor, 1987; Rhodes, 1981; Tompkins & Webeler, 1983) and the benefits of predictability during reading. Predictable texts were generally juxtaposed against the "contrived, unnatural sentences of basal primers" (Bridge, *et al.,* 1983, p.884). Predictable elements gave young readers some sense of control over the multiple cues of the test, and often the playful language of the pattern had some function in the text as a whole. I suspect that the spiritedness and the tale-weaving of good predictable texts draw readers into the experience of reading.

Unfortunately, when patterned texts were translated into Canadian basals, in many cases the pattern often took precedence over playfulness and function. Although the following examples include patterned language, they are not very engaging and the pattern has little function in the text.

> Here is my hat.
> It is orange.
> Here is my T-shirt.
> It is red . . . . (Booth, 1984, p.4–5)

> In school today
> my teacher said,
> "Welcome, Brad.
> I like your smile."
> I think my teacher likes me . . . (McInnes, 1986, p.6)

When patterned texts were translated into Canadian basals, in many cases the pattern often took precedence over playfulness and function.

These authors have taken the notion of pattern and have used it to create what Unsworth and Williams (1988) call "engineered texts." The primary purpose of engineered text is repetition of text elements. Of course, this was the same rationale for the contrived nature of the Dick and Jane era. Engineered patterned texts comprise twelve percent of the selections in first-grade Canadian basals. This percentage seems small. Given the abundance of high-quality patterned language children's literature that is available, however, I question why any engineered selections remain.

In fact, engineered text of a different type pervades Canadian basals. In four out of the five programs I examined, nearly 70 percent of the first-grade texts were written by basal employees. Only Holt reprinted excerpts from tradebooks on a large scale. This high proportion of in-house-written texts suggests that Canadian publishers still feel some need to control textual material in order to teach young children to read. The in-house texts have short sentences and words with few syllables without concern for the effects of these constraints on a young reader's understanding of that text. Goodman (1987) suggests that reducing the amount of text that young students read in first grade often makes the comprehension of passages more difficult because much of the context for reading has been eroded. Ironically, the contextual supports that could make texts more "predictable" and would involve young readers in an integrated use of the cueing systems of language are often bypassed as basal authors struggle with the contradictions of creating texts for teaching and for reading.

At McGraw-Hill, the control of the text is so great that a series of texts in one book contains the same number of pages, each page has the same number of sentences, each sentence has the same number of words, and each word is close to the same number of syllables.

The brown deer can run.
Deer run in the woods. (Rennick, *et al.*, 1984c, p.34)
The white horse can run.
Horses run at the farm. (Rennick, *et al.*, 1984a, p.42)
The blue bird can fly.
Birds fly in the city. (Rennick, *et al.*, 1984b, p.50)

By third and fifth grades, the number of in-house-written texts decreases significantly. However, the high incidence at the first-grade level contradicts the ascription of the term "anthology" to Canadian basals because that term typically denotes a collection of literary works by different authors.

Authority Over Teaching

Basals, like any other tool, can be used in many ways. However, few tools come with manuals as explicit as the basal teacher's manual. In these manuals are the publishers' recommendations about how teachers should use their materials. Just as the engineered stories attempt to control students' reading, the Canadian basal teacher's manuals attempt to control teachers' teaching. For example, in the Canadian basals, publishers often organize stories, poems, and informational texts into themes and then organize the themes into discrete lessons. Although all publishers provide lists of suggested readings outside of the basal for each theme, they do not cross reference other basal themes. This suggests that publishers still have not abandoned the idea that the sequence of stories in basals must be followed from first to last page in order to teach students to read. Nelson has come up with software to enable teachers to make such cross references themselves, but only on a limited basis. Yet, even Nelson's manual reflects a tightly controlled process for theme development that mocks the open-ended process in which teachers and students work together to construct themes.

The teacher is implicitly portrayed as being without "authority" for literacy education.

This subtle intent to control instruction is made explicit in the language of the teacher's manual. In all Canadian basals, publishers use directive language to explain lessons. Teachers are told to "provide," "repeat," "read" specific parts of the text, and "show" specific items. Such language conveys certainty to teachers, suggesting that successful teaching is like cooking by following all the directions of a recipe. No wonder Shannon (1989) argues that teachers often believe that the basals do the teaching. Despite this directive language in lessons, McGraw-Hill does discuss some of its components more tentatively—"a suggested approach to this story and song" or "suggested types of questions" (Rennick *et al.*, 1985, p. 48). Moreover, McGraw-Hill, Nelson, and Holt include general teaching strategies at the beginning of each manual in language that suggest a sharing among knowledgeable professionals rather than directives from superiors. This collegiality is spoiled, however, by the directive stance in each lesson.

In summary, most of the time Canadian teacher's manuals are just that—manuals for teaching. The teacher is implicitly portrayed as being without "authority" for literacy education. Sometimes, the manuals come closer to the notion of source books or guides. At best, the manuals reflect a transition from one type of literacy instruction to another, but currently, those manuals send teachers a mixed message about who is in charge of the literacy program.

Workbooks

Compared to the United States' workbooks reviewed in the *Report Card on Basal Readers*, Canadian workbooks look wonderful. Yet, appearances are deceiving. In a study of the use of Holt *Impressions* in classrooms, Johnson *et al.* (1987) named the theoretical gap between Holt workbooks and the rest of their program. Hayden (1991) expanded this critique to other Canadian basals. He found that while all Canadian publishers include "real text" in their workbooks, there is little uniformity across series or grade levels. He found that only Nelson provides workbook assignments that support "the students' understanding that print is used for purposeful endeavors" (p.142). The open-ended appearance of Canadian workbooks can be attributed to each publishers' demand that students produce text rather than copy or circle text. However, Hayden cautions that this production does not necessarily mean that these exercises have a purpose outside of workbook completion. Real texts without real purposes suggest that the workbooks do embody the contradictions of the Canadian basals.

Thoughtful Evaluation

Evaluation procedures are the greatest difference between Canadian and United States basals. Canadian basal publishers trust teachers and students. Unlike their United States counterparts, Canadian basals do not include basal tests of any kind as program components. There are no end-of-unit, -level, or -book tests, nor are there theme tests or process tests that characterize the new United States basals (See Murphy, Chapter 7). Rather, Canadian publishers opt to provide supportive information and materials to assist teachers in gathering data on the students' reading development in their classrooms. In some cases, the publishers recommend forms and procedures for students to engage in self-evaluation. In all basals, variations of miscue analysis (Goodman, 1982; Goodman, Watson, & Burke, 1987) are used as methods for assessing reading. Observational guides are provided to aid teachers in their assessment of students' everyday literacy activities. Each publisher offers

By providing suggestions, and not tests, Canadian publishers return some authority to teachers.

forms so that students can react and respond to the texts as they read them. By providing suggestions, and not tests, Canadian publishers return some authority to teachers and students in the teaching of reading. They trust that teachers will use their professional knowledge to interpret the indicators of literacy and that students can provide systematic reflection of their own literacy to help in their evaluation.

THE SOCIAL CONTEXT OF CANADIAN BASALS

Canadian basals are hybrids. They retain vestiges of the traditional basals, but they have made some effort to shift toward more progressive views of literacy. Of course, some publishers have been more successful than others in these efforts. This hybrid form may be partially explained by educational publishing cycles in Canada. Canadian basals do not go through the five- or six-year cycle for new editions that United States publishers follow. It is not uncommon for Canadian basals to be in use with a publication date more than a decade old. This difference relates to the economics of introducing basal programs into a market one-tenth the size of the United States. Consequently, publishers cannot make rapid changes in basals in order to meet the trends in literacy research and theory, even if they want to.

The market for Canadian basals is complex. Canadian provinces "authorize," "approve," or "recommend" a text or series for use in school. For instance, Ontario annually approves a list of texts (see, for example, Ontario Ministry of Education, 1991) that school boards are required to provide to students without charge. The districts must purchase all books for their students. However, in language arts, "reading and reference material, including novels, periodicals, plays, short stories, single-genre anthologies and dictionaries do not require Ministry approval" (Ontario Ministry of Education, 1991, p. x). That is, the districts can choose to purchase books that do not appear on the list and distribute them instead of basals to their students. In Newfoundland, however, a single basal series is "authorized" for all schools. This means that the province provides these basals to schools free of charge. Moreover, the use of other programs or texts must be approved by the Ministry of Education in that province and must be paid for by the school district itself. For economic reasons, then authorization is close to a mandate.

What's in store for Canadian basals? Malicky (1990) and Cameron and Mickelson (1989) charge that whole language has been basalized in Canadian programs. Yet, Gordon (1991) claims that in a climate generally favorable toward holistic instruction "basal programs are no longer thought of as complete language arts programs even if they do combine all aspects of the language arts rather than just focusing on teaching reading" (p.153–154). Such a climate may force publishers to play catch-up with the current holistic educational trends while trying to preserve their markets in more conservative areas. In this case, we can anticipate that basals will continue to improve despite occasional contradictions. However, if recent national press, which favors the "back to basics" movement, and the national testing movement are any indication of things to come, it is just as likely that the traditional elements of basals will again dominate. Given that the cycle for new editions will shortly draw to a close for most Canadian basals, it will be interesting to see whether "basalized whole language" will evolve into something even more progressive or whether basals will succumb to the pressures of a conservative educational press and move even closer to their United States counterparts.

10

HEARTS AND MINDS AND LITERACY: LESSONS FROM OURSELVES

MEM FOX

I don't look like a soldier. I carry no guns and I'm not dressed in battle fatigues, but I'm fighting. I'm fighting a battle on behalf of the development of literacy. As a peace-child of the 1960s I'm unhappy about using the metaphor of war, but in my current state of passion I see no purpose in making peace with groups of people whose idleness or financial self-interest is killing literacy, or at least causing its stunted growth. Politeness has hitherto proven to be ineffective so I have decided, from now on, not to water down my remarks. I intend to write from the heart and with feeling.

My adversaries in the trenches across the barbed wire are education professors and reading specialists who haven't kept up-to-date, and educational publishers who produce basal readers designed specifically to teach reading and writing. I'll begin by setting my sights on the publishers.

Don't publishers realize how embarrassingly out of date they are?

Publishers continue to provide us with less-than-effective basal readers and waste-of-time worksheets that meet neither our needs as literacy teachers, nor our children's needs as literacy learners. I thought we'd told them long ago that we didn't want basal readers anymore, yet there are always millions of basals on display at conventions such as the International Reading Association (IRA). I thought we'd told publishers long ago that we didn't want questions and word lists and activities in the books we use with children, yet there are millions of mindless questions, pointless word lists, and unambitious activities in reading and writing books published every day. Don't publishers realize how embarrassingly out of date they are? Are they deaf that they do not hear?

One reason for the slow learning about literacy and the best ways of developing it might be that teachers have been too sweet, too polite, or too muted in their demands. Perhaps publishers would have acceded more quickly to their requests if teachers had started protesting earlier and more forcefully. Perhaps they would have acceded more quickly to teachers' demands if teachers had stood up for themselves by vigorously challenging the odious assumption that publishers know more than teachers do about children and the way they become literate.

We teachers *do* know what is required. Our knowledge comes from common sense reflection on the daily experiences and interactions we have with children in our homes and in our classrooms. But will they listen, these publishers? Will they listen? Pardon my screaming on the page, but I have come to believe that only screams will be heard.

What we want is real books written for children. Note that there are only seven words in our request: that's all. There's nothing tagged onto that sentence. We did not say: "We want books for children, but make sure they are specially designed by educators who adhere to the behaviorist school of psychology

because we want these books to have special vocabularies at carefully graded levels, with word lists, activities and questions at the end of every chapter." Our request is not 47 words long, it's a mere seven words long:
"We•want•real•books•written•for•children."

And we want millions of them, literally millions;
huge print-runs that will lower publishing costs and
our spending costs. If only the billions of dollars put
into the publication of vile basals could be spent instead on producing real books: marvelous books,
funny books, beautiful books, nonsexist books, sad
books, gross books, nonfiction books, gentle books,
noisy books, heroic books, science fiction books, fan-
tasy books, nonracist books, romance books, animal
books, poetry books, scary books, foreign books, classic books, any books, as long as they're *real* books:
one-at-a-time books, not bunched together in thick,
heavy textbooks. And we want them pure—don't
we?—without graded levels, without questions,
without activities, and without deadening ditto
sheets.

At this point I ought to pause before repositioning
myself in the trenches to ask whether I should assume
that I can speak on behalf of all teachers. It may be
that there still remain teachers so poorly equipped to
teach that they are at a loss as to what to do with
real children's books. There may be teachers who still
believe that plain, unadulterated, real children's
books do not provide sufficient material in themselves
for the successful mastery of reading. There may still
exist teachers who feel lost without the scaffolding of
questions and words lists and teachers' guides that
publishers provide. Don't get me wrong. I'm not
blaming the teachers—I'm blaming the college professors who trained them. I'm one of this questionable
group. I'm not blameless myself, but I do hope I practice what I'm about to preach more often than not.

It seems to me that much of current preservice
teacher training is so controlled by publishers that

Are we creating teachers who are wide awake and wonderfully critical?

teachers are being taught merely how to use the inadequate materials available in schools instead being fired up with all the latest theories of best practice—theories that challenge such material and challenge the school boards who buy it and the uninformed parents who insist on its use.

We teacher educators need to look deep within ourselves and ask: Are we creating teachers who are wide awake and wonderfully critical, able to teach creatively without basals or worksheets, knowledgeable about children's books and different theories of language learning and teaching, and very confident in their practice? Are we? My own sad observations reveal that too many teachers are uncertain of themselves and their methods. Their uncertainty stems from clashes between their own common sense hunches about the teaching of literacy and what they are told to do by so-called curriculum experts. They lack a solid foundation of exciting theory. Their creativity has been stifled at teachers' colleges. They feel they know nothing and that college professors and publishers know everything. And the assumption of many of those college professors and publishers—that school teachers are too stupid to be capable of critical thought and therefore have to be spoon-fed—has left them with a crippling lack of confidence. I believe it's time a few teacher educators went back to school and learned some creativity and new ideas themselves.

Is it any wonder, given the training of teachers and the power of publishers, that so many teachers are frightened to think for themselves, that so many teachers lack self-esteem? Is it any wonder so many teachers meekly do as they are told, which is to open the teacher's handbook, give workbooks and basals to the children, tinker at the edges of the curriculum, hope for the best, and pick up their paycheck at the end of the month? If nothing else, I hope, at least in this chapter, to raise the self-concept of the teachers and to provide sufficient ammunition for them to fight their own battles against inappropriate or inadequate published material; to arm them with confidence in their own capabilities and provide them with enough educational and literary dynamite to storm the published barricades in their own schools and school districts.

Before I continue to fire from every barrel I should begin to clarify the difference as I see it between what I call "real" books and those books written with a teaching purpose in mind. I'll share a few texts (several short ones and one slightly longer) and dissect them to show their inner workings and assess their efficacy as material for the teaching of reading. Let me begin with a book that will be familiar to us all, at least in the general sense:

> Nip finds a red tin.
> He hides in the red tin.
> Daddy will not find Nip in the red tin.
> Dick hides in a tree in the park.
> Fluff hides in a tree too.
> Mummy and Dora hide by the hut.
> Jack gets into a sack in the hut.
> You cannot see Jack in the big sack.
> Daddy goes to find them all (Schonell, 1972).

The mind-numbingly dull Nip and Fluff, Dick and Dora series was first published in Australia during the early 1950s and incredibly, was still being reprinted in the mid-1970s. The extent of the terrible damage this series wreaked upon the literacy levels of those who suffered them is too distressing to contemplate. If that was *reading* who would have wanted to learn to read? Why would they have wanted to?

And here's another series from the 1970s. I'll be able to read the whole book in ten seconds.

> Michael likes to play ball.
> Paul likes to watch football.
> Dad takes Paul and Michael to football.
> They all watch football (Fischer, *et al*, 1972).

Basals offer no reward whatsoever for inquisitive, eager minds.

This time the dozy, incompetent authors had finally woken up to the fact that the topic had to be of some interest to children. But they had forgotten or didn't realize that *the way it was written* also had to be interesting. Subject matter alone isn't enough to ignite the spark of reading.

These texts and those like them have much to answer for. Given the hideous nature of such material and the fact that it's swilling around our schools we shouldn't be surprised that there are so many unhappy, emasculated, unemployed, ashamed, unemployable illiterates, and semi-literates in our cities, on our streets, in our schools, in our prisons, in our gangs, in our middle class suburbs, and even in our master's degree programs. Basals offer no reward whatsoever for inquisitive, eager minds. Children reading this filth groan and moan and fidget their way through it, developing unfortunate but understandably negative attitudes to reading at the turn of every page.

Thanks to Frank Smith, and the research of Kenneth Goodman and Yetta Goodman and others, we've known for many years that the act of competent reading involves a great deal of constant, on-the-hop prediction. It's a major part of the real reading process. The better we can predict what's coming in the text the less we need to focus on every word that's printed. We focus on the print only when the material is unfamiliar and is therefore more difficult to skim over. Our predictions are based on three sources of knowledge: what we know about *language* and the way it works; what we know about the *world* and how it works; and what we know about the *print on the page* and how that works. The more we know about how language works, how the world works, and how print works the better, faster readers we become.

We also know, by listening to them, that most English-speaking five-year-olds know how English works. When they speak, they construct most English sentences correctly, using normal grammatical patterns. When they read they naturally expect those normal patterns of English to be reproduced in print. They expect that one thing will lead to another logically, especially if they're familiar with fairy stories, picture book texts or even the anecdotes told by older members of the family. In the pattern of a story, first one thing happens and then because of that, another thing happens, and then another, and so on until the story reaches a resolution of some kind. So children expect in books, as in life, that there'll be a sense of continuing cause and effect. Where, I ask, is the cause and effect in:

> Michael likes to play ball.
> Paul likes to watch football.
> Dad takes Paul and Michael to football.
> They all watch football (Fischer, *et al.*, 1972)?

Children also expect stories to be in the past tense. I've always been tremendously puzzled by the fact that the writers of first-grade basals could be so idiotically ignorant that they didn't know stories are usually written in the past. Past tense is natural language. When children read real stories they naturally seek past tense indicators such as *was* and *were* and *did* and *said* and their predictions are justified. Real books are not *more* difficult to read than basals—they're actually much easier to read than basals because language works in the normal, expected manner.

Basals create other problems as well that I'll mention after my next exciting read-aloud from two different basals. Note the present tense. Note also the lack of all those elements that I consider to be prerequisites for turning children onto books: the lack of emotion; the lack of exquisite language; the lack of character development; the lack of tension; the lack of plot; and the complete lack of predictability in both the language and the story. Note, in fact, the lack of a *single* redeeming quality. The first book is called *Lost at Football:*

> After dinner dad takes Paul and Michael to the football.
> Dad looks for his money.
> Michael sees a man with a big red rattle.
> He goes to the big red rattle.
> Dad looks down.
> Michael is lost.
> The man sees Michael crying and lifts him up.
> Dad sees Michael.
> They all watch football (Fischer, *et al.*, 1972).

The second book is *Michael's Bump:*

> After school Michael and Paul play in the park.
> They go up the big slide.
> They play on the swings.
> Michael falls off the swings and bumps his head.
> Mum takes Michael to the hospital.
> A doctor looks at his bump.
> A nurse puts a bandage on his head.
> Mum takes him home (Fischer, *et al.*, 1972).

There is little cause and effect in these basals. Predictions are confounded time and time again. As readers we could surely be forgiven for predicting that after: "Dad looks down. Michael is lost," the next sentence might say something like: "Dad is frantic," or: "Dad looks for him." Instead we have: "Michael is lost. The man sees Michael crying and lifts him up."

In *Michael's Bump* the story starts in the present tense, which is perfectly acceptable: "After school Michael and Paul play in the park. They go up the big slide. They play on the swings." Any reader accustomed to the way stories work would then expect a change in the tense: 'One day, when Michael was on the swings . . ." But no. The present tense *incorrectly* continues: "Michael falls off the swings and bumps his head. Mum takes Michael to the hospital."

Apart from their crazy tenses, both of these books,

and all the basals like them fall into what I call the "well-so-what?" category. We read them and think: "Well, so what?" Kids read them and think: "Well, so what?" When I'm feeling tired at the end of a hard day I don't run a bubble bath and with a delicious sense of anticipation ease myself into the warm bubbles and read a basal. I've never read a "well-so-what?" book by choice or for pleasure—the very idea is preposterous. Their interest level is zero and the teaching they provide is far more negative than positive.

Kids read them and think: "Well, so what?"

I have traveled a great deal in the past year and met many people. I have been to Pakistan and witnessed horrors there; I've had an intimate conversation with a twelve-year-old girl in the Carolinas who was raped not long before I arrived; I have visited glass-blowers in England and learned about their craft; I have listened with fascination to an intelligent woman who thought she was a man; I have been to Mexico and learned new recipes; I have been taught good manners by an old friend; I have walked with Einstein in Switzerland and shared his dreams. There was no physical movement nor jet-lag involved: I had all these experiences and met all these people in the books I have read.

What an interesting pleasure it was to travel in time and place so extensively and to meet such a mad variety of characters! And as I read, of course, I picked up styles and nuances, words and ideas, themes and stories that improved my own writing when I next sat down to write. What fantastic wealth I receive from reading!

And what poverty children receive from basals: always the same bland people; always the same bland plot; always the same bland period of time—here and now; always the same bland kinds of words, never ever the richness of language and experience that would hook them into books, thereby making them better readers and writers.

I believe basal readers are the greatest single cause of illiteracy.

The bizarre use of language in basals makes them unsuitable for any classroom. They confuse children and make learning to read extremely and unnaturally difficult. No wonder Jenny and Johnny can't read! And no wonder they can't write either. What kind of models do these books provide for young writers? Readers of basals actually receive *wrong* messages about writing. They are provided with innumerable incorrect and inelegant examples of the written forms of our language. For this reason in particular, basals should never be used with second language learners or with children having difficulty in learning to read.

Yet publishers keep selling basals and teachers keep buying them in the belief that children can only learn to read by reading graded texts written specifically to teach reading. In spite of the current rate of illiteracy! Isn't it incredible that in the developed countries with the lowest rates of literacy, educators continue to insist upon the use of basals—a product that fails, and fails again? Isn't it criminal? Isn't it stupid? Isn't it simply *unbelievable?* Imagine attempting to buy a make of car in which the brakes had been proven to be faulty. Even if we wanted to buy such a car we wouldn't be able to: the car manufacturer would have taken all the cars of that type off the road immediately. But not basals. These educational pests are permitted to remain with us, resolutely eating away at literacy while we look the other way and pretend not to notice.

I believe basal readers are the greatest single cause of illiteracy. I believe that basals are so criminally destructive they should be indicted on the grounds of literary and educational abuse. I believe publishers should shudder with shame for slowing down the development of literacy in the English speaking world since it was they who highjacked the curriculum and dared to say, "We know best!" all those years ago. I believe if basals were banned tomorrow and only real books were allowed in classrooms, illiteracy would be wiped out in one generation. But are governments and school districts listening? Are the publishers listening? And if so, do they hear?

The answer is yes. Some publishers are listening and they do hear, but their response is not always quite as intelligent as we would like it to be. They get the message that we want real books so they approach those of us who already write real books for children, on the assumption that our names on the covers will inspire great confidence in those who buy them. But here is a moral tale . . .

In the early 1980s I was asked if I would write books for a new reading scheme. The praiseworthy aim of the publishers was to provide children with books that were real, written by real authors who would use the real and natural language of texts. The overall concept thrilled me, but I told the publisher the truth—that I cannot write to order, have never been able to write to order, and would never write to order because I believe a good story has to be organic, rising out of my soul, out of the gurgling compost of experiences and emotions that have made me who I am.

"Oh dear," said the publishers, for they admitted they were anxious to have my name on their publicity material, "are you sure you won't write for us?"

"Quite sure," I replied.

They thought a while and came back to me.

"Do you have anything in your bottom drawer?" they asked. "Anything rejected by other publishers, perhaps? Anything suitable for early reading?"

I was a little disturbed by the ethics of the situation. If my rejected manuscripts hadn't been good enough to be real books how could they suddenly be good enough for a reading scheme? Were children going to be tricked into believing they were real books? Yes, they were. Even so, in a moment of weakness that I regret with all my heart, I sent off three rejected manuscripts, all of which were published. These and others are the "pathetic" books that appear in the American title of my autobiography: *Dear Mem Fox I*

*What's the
purpose in turning
the page?*

Have Read All Your Books, Even the Pathetic Ones. I'll share one and then say what's wrong with it. It's called *Zoo Looking:*

> One day Effie went to the zoo.
> She looked at the lion.
> And the lion looked back.
> She looked at the tiger
> With the stripes across his back.
> She looked at the bear
> And the bear looked back.
> She looked at the crocodile
> Whose tail went "Whack!"
> She looked at the zebra
> And the zebra looked back.
> She looked at the monkey
> As its baby got a smack.
> She looked at the parrot
> And the parrot looked back.
> She looked at the koala
> With a baby on its back.
> She looked at the gorilla
> And the gorilla looked back.
> She looked at the elephant
> Next to the yak.
> She looked at the walrus
> And the walrus looked back.
> She looked at the duck
> And it went, 'Quack!"
> She looked at her dad
> And he smiled back (Fox, 1986).

Honestly, so what? I mean, *so what?* All right, so it has some predictability. So it's written in the past tense. So it may be of enormous interest to a two-year-old—but, hey, aren't school kids at least five years old and over? What I want to know is where's the tension? Where's the reason to read? Where's that most important element in the teaching of reading: the emotional pull of the text? What's the purpose in turning the page? Where's the beautiful language?

Where's the sort of *Wilfrid-Gordon-McDonald-Partridge*-depth that will cause the book to be remembered with fondness into adulthood? Would a child voluntarily return to this book and re-read it over and over? No.

Zoo Looking is not a real book even though my name is on the cover. It didn't arise out of a well of feeling and I didn't rewrite it over many months and years with loving care. I think it would be brutal but fair to say that with a few notable exceptions like Margaret Mahy and Joy Cowley most writers of basals are second rate. They couldn't get a real book published if they tried. Why do first-rate writers bother to write for basal schemes? Perhaps they, like me, receive letters from New York like this one, which arrived in mid-January, 1993:

> [We are] developing a library of 4-color books for a major publisher of educational materials. The target reader is approximately 6-years-old, in first grade, and just learning to read.
> We are soliciting fiction and non-fiction manuscripts from well-known authors who have published for this audience. The deadline is _____ and we would need your manuscript by _____.
> We hope you will be interested in participating in this innovative program.

This particular letter aroused my deepest suspicions. I thought it might be merely my name they wanted ("We are soliciting . . . manuscripts from *well-known* authors . . . ") not necessarily a good manuscript for a real book. I sighed and decided to wreak my revenge.

"You pesky publishers," I said. "I'll show you!" and with a friend I spent a couple of hours one afternoon laughing and giggling and writing terrible texts to send away, wondering if they would be accepted on the basis of my name. One of them was *"No way," said Fay*.

In classrooms we need texts published and designed for the children's market, not the school market.

"Come and play," said Ray.
"No way!" said Fay.
"Come and skip," said Pip.
"No way!" said Fay.
"Play ball?" said Paul.
"No way!" said Fay.
"Roller skate?" said Kate.
"No way!" said Fay.
"Like a swim?" said Jim.
"No way!" said Fay.
"Let's draw," said Lenore.
"No way!" said Fay.
"TV?" said Bee.
"No way!" said Fay.
Her friends stood there, all together, staring.
"Why not?" they said.
        "Because," said Fay, "I'm READING!"

I'm happy to report it was rejected. They were all rejected, thank heaven! There are some sensible publishers out there after all. Had they accepted my manuscripts I would have withdrawn my permission for them to be published. Even if I had made an effort and had successfully written texts suitable for basal readers they would not have been good enough, not really: they *could not have been* good enough because they would have been written to order, not from the reality of a deep desire to say something that needs saying. (I did apologize for wasting the time of the perceptive publisher who rejected them.)

I told this story of mine as a timely warning to those who purchase the texts for any class, school, or district. Please don't let yourselves be fooled by publishers who claim their program is a cut above the rest simply because it has famous children's authors writing its texts. Look at the actual texts first. Some of them might pass the "Well, so what? test, but my earnest advice would be to be suspicious of any text in a set that's been published and designed specifically for the school market. In classrooms we need

texts published and designed for the children's market, not the school market. There's a quantum leap
of difference between the two.

Let me expand further on this distinction by focusing on a particular real book because I think it will
demonstrate the qualities that differentiate "real"
from "basal" better than I can. Unlike basals, this
book was written for children, not for schools. It was
written with anguish over the horrors of war, not with
anal anxiety over the horrors of phonics. Unlike a
basal, it has story worth telling, with tension that
builds to breaking point. Unlike a basal, it leaves its
readers changed by the experience of having read it.
Unlike a basal, it has no controlled vocabulary. It's
written in the past tense using normal English (translated from the original Japanese) and it asks readers to
predict intelligently its frightful outcome. Ted Lewin's
illustrations are evocative, and supportive of the tone
of the story. It smells nice. And physically, it's the
right size and weight for children to hold.

The book is *Faithful Elephants, A True Story of Animals, People and War*, written by Yukio Tsuchiya. It is
the true story of the animals at Ueno Zoo in Tokyo
during World War II who had to be killed in case
the zoo was bombed and they ran amok. It was so
physically difficult to kill the beloved elephants that
after many different attempts, much to the distress of
the keepers, they had to be starved to death. All the
while the frantic keepers hoped the war would end
before the elephants died so they could feed them
again, but the war did not end in time. The bombs
continued to rain down and the three elephants died
agonizingly slow, confused, and tragic deaths.

It's a heart-rending story and a treasure trove of
emotion, experience, and language! But already I can
hear a voice saying, "I wouldn't read that to children.
It's much too sad, much too graphic." For heaven's
sake! Children are tougher than most of us realize and
cope better and more matter-of-factly than adults do

with this kind of story. Please! The things they see and hear elsewhere in their lives are far more horrifying than *Faithful Elephants*. To deny them the experience of this book on the grounds that it's too sad for them suggests a generational lack of understanding of today's children and their needs.

And if they weep with us as we read, so much the better. Something in print will have touched them at last. Something in print will have made them aware—perhaps for the first time—that within the pages of a book it is occasionally possible to discover a story worth thinking about, a story with an impact that lasts for years rather than minutes, a story that makes reading seem like a possible attraction rather than a likely chore. It's the stories that make us think and feel, laugh aloud or cry, gasp or shiver, snuggle in, or want to share that which makes us *want* to read and keep on reading. The more we read the more we learn how to read effectively. For this reason also, basals are ineffective: even when they succeed tortuously to teach decoding skills they never create that all-important *desire* to read.

Crying seems to me to be one of the most important things for teachers to do in front of their classes, now and then, because it is the best possible testament to the power of literature. Teachers who are seen by their students to cry and laugh over books are creating the most enticing invitations to read. They are promising their students that magic lies between book covers—the sort of incredible magic that can make even a teacher lose her composure for a while. (Good grief!) So of course I find it disturbing and disappointing when teachers say to me:

"I can't read *Wilfrid Gordon McDonald Partridge* in front of the class. I can't get through it without crying. I have to leave the room."

Leave the room??? Stop the kids from learning one of the most important lessons of all?—That reading has an effect, and that's why people do it, and that's why people love it, and why there's some point in learning to read? Dear oh dear! What's the problem? Are teachers supposed to role-play being sub-human from 9 AM to 3 PM? Are they so used to the deadening effect of basals (which have never made anyone laugh or cry) that they're frightened to be real in front of the class when they read real books? Are these teachers nervous about loss of face, or what? Loss of discipline? If so, what on earth is happening to classroom relationships? What sort of false, unnatural learning environment are teachers and their pupils being constrained by? Surely we should allow them to read and enjoy books together, not apart; to read *with* each other, not *at* each other. To share the drama and excitement of literature, not to keep it to themselves.

Reading is associated with love and warmth, with noise and fun.

Picture the sharing that occurs in a home when a doting parent reads aloud to a book-hungry preschool child. There's the thrill of anticipation about the literary component of the shared reading: "OOH, I can't *wait* to listen to this story again!" and there's the thrill of being close to a loved member of the family: "OOH, I just *love* being snuggled up beside Poppy!" Reading is associated with love and warmth, with noise and fun, with joys and sorrows, with secrets and laughter, with questions and answers and the scrumptious richness of memories. Can we replicate the deliciousness of this loving, sharing atmosphere in our classrooms? Of course we can, as long as we read real books and remain true to our real selves.

Writers who keep that bedtime scene in mind as they write, who agonize over words in order to create shared joys, sit down to write with a completely different intention from writers of basals. Writers who write for parents and children—let's call them "the joy writers"—face the blank page with a heart full of love, and a determination to provide exciting destinations for the pursuit of happiness. Their emotional and literary aim is to please, not to teach—an aim that makes terrible demands and takes it toll. A joy writer might take days to find the right name for a character; months to perfect a sentence; and years to make a story sound just right. A joy writer struggles long and hard against the cantankerousness of the blank page.

The writers of basals, on the other hand, sit down to write with a bitter Calvinistic intention: "OK, let's get these little tigers to learn to read." Their hearts are empty of literary warmth. Concentrating on the superficial tedium and irrelevance of individual words and letter combinations they set to work to produce texts to teach, rather than texts to please. They forget, or do not know, that the books that please are the books that make the little tigers literate. The books that please are the real books, and the real books are the best teachers of all.

When I'm asked by puzzled teachers: "What's *real*, Mem? How do you know what a *real* book is? What is the litmus test?" I often say: "Read the book; then put yourself inside the writer's head. Ask why the writer wrote the book. If it was to teach, it's not a real book. If it was to please, it is a real book because it was written by a joy writer."

My most recent book is a real book, not a basal, because I kept the bedtime scene in mind while I was writing it, and I wrote it with a full heart, as a joy writer, intending to please. I recalled the nights when my daughter Chloë was very little and lively and wide awake and wicked about going to bed. I recalled how tired my husband and I used to be and how wearily patient we were with all the bedtime rituals, the cajoling and the book reading, the kisses and the night lights, the chatting and the night-time drink, and *the way none of it worked*. I guessed that there were parents all over the world with children like mine and I pitied them. I hoped my book would please those parents at bedtime. And I hoped my words would dreamily hypnotize their children to sleep. It's called *Time for Bed* and begins:

It's time for bed, little mouse, little mouse,
Darkness is falling all over the house.

*

It's time for bed, little goose, little goose,
The stars are out and on the loose.

*

It's time for bed, little cat, little cat,
So snuggle in tight, that's right, like that.

*

It's time for bed, little calf, little calf,
What happened today that made you laugh?

*

It's time for bed, little foal, little foal,
I'll whisper a secret, but don't tell a soul . . .

*

The structure of *Time for Bed* is the kind of structure we might find in a basal. It's written in rhyming couplets, like *Zoo Looking*, using simple, easy-to-read words. It has the repetition of sight vocabulary in: "It's time for bed" and: "It's time to sleep." The word "little" could well have been a focus word for a basal writer whose reason for including it 24 times would have been for the tiresome purpose of grapho-phonic reinforcement and consolidation.

The similarities between *Time for Bed* and a basal are obvious. The differences are less clear. The least visible and most important difference between it and a text like *"No way!" said Fay* is what went on inside my head as I sat down to write each one. If a teacher or parent were to read both books and ask: "What was Mem Fox's *intention* in each case: to please or to teach?" I hope he or she would realize that *Time for Bed* is meant to please and *"No way! said Fay* was meant to teach. And having come to that realization I hope *"No way!" said Fay* would be thrown into the back of a cupboard to grow moldy in the mists of time.

The other important difference between these two books is their tone. There's a hastiness and lack of warmth in *"No way!" said Fay*, whereas *Time for Bed* has a genuine tenderness which carries with it the potential to bond children to books, parents to children and books to parents. This threesome relationship is far more important to reading development than the controlled vocabularies of basals. A wild enthusiasm for books shared by children, their parents, and their teachers, creates a desire to read, and a desire to learn to read.

Does that ever happen with a basal? Did anyone ever hear of a *basal* that kindled a desire to read? Does a basal exist so filled with love and tenderness that parents have borrowed it to read to their children at bedtime? Does one teacher ever rave enthusiastically to another about a basal some kid happened to bring in that morning?

What would happen if all the basals in the world were thrown out tomorrow? First, all the poorly trained teachers would be thrown into a panic because they've never been given the theory or creative practice to develop a reading-writing curriculum of their own. The answer to that problem might be to retrain the trainers: the college professors who teach teachers, but that would take too long.

Another answer might be to continue doggedly to live in the past. After all, it's very easy to "basalize" real books by continuing to write worksheets filled with the usual inane comprehension questions about the real books read in class:

1. How many elephants were there in the book *Faithful Elephants?* [Who cares? I loved the book. It made me cry and I now detest war even more than I did before.]
2. What were the elephants' names? [Who cares? I loved the book. It made me cry and I now detest war even more than I did before.]
3. In which city is Ueno Zoo? [Who cares? I loved the book. It made me cry and I now detest war even more than I did before.]

4. Were the other animals shot or poisoned? [Who cares? I loved the book. It made me cry and I now detest war even more than I did before.]
5. How many days did it take for the elephants to die? [Who cares? I loved the book. It made me cry and I now detest war even more than I did before.]

We all know from current experience or the dim memories of our own childhoods that it's possible to answer comprehension questions correctly without ever having read the passage. Worksheets do not test reading skills. Instead they militate *against* reading development by encouraging readers *not* to engage in the mesmerizing wonder of the wholeness of texts. They are in effect saying, "Hey kids, don't bother to read. Don't be dumb. There's an easier way out. Read the question first, *then* read the text. Just get the answer, don't bother with the meaning."

Perhaps basalizing real books would *not* be the best thing to do after we have thrown out the basals. The very idea of basalizing literature, especially my own, could give me a massive heart attack and I'm not ready to die.

If we can't retrain professors and we can't basalize books, what can we do? We could always choose to starve, of course, and spend all our pennies on real books so we could read aloud to our students all day. This would certainly be enormously beneficial to our students' progress in the literacy stakes, but it might be slightly difficult to justify the *"all* day" bit to our superiors.

I guess we might be able to find a charismatic leader to take us into the streets in our thousands shouting: "What do we want? Good ideas! When do we want them? Now! What do we want? Good ideas! When do we want them? Now!" but it would take a lot of time and organization and what if it were educational

We have to trust ourselves to be able to reflect deeply and sensibly in our own reading, writing, listening, and speaking.

publishers who answered our call? Surely that's the last thing we would want.

Is there any solution? Is there any life after basals? Of course there is. As real readers and writers we need to start thinking for ourselves instead of allowing professors and publishers to think for us. We should be analyzing what *we* enjoy as readers and why; how *we* learn best and why; what *we* write, and how, and why; and which conditions are the best for writing, and what are the processes we go through. If we looked at our own lives we would discover the immediate reality that we never read basals or fill in worksheets. We would discover the reality that when we finish reading a book we have loved, all we want to do is to tell someone else about it as soon as possible. We have to trust ourselves to be able to reflect deeply and sensibly in our own reading, writing, listening, and speaking in order to be able to teach it to others.

All we have to do is what teachers have already done successfully in the thousands of schools all over the world from which basals have been removed, Finland and New Zealand being the most shining examples. We need to "get real." We need to introduce connected, whole realities of language to replace the disconnected, pointless bits that currently litter our curriculum. We need real writing, real books, and real relationships. We need real help and cooperation from fellow teachers who are experienced in and excited about whole language. We need in-service programs and up-to-date professional texts. We need the courage to make mistakes, for without them how will we learn?

Perhaps, above all, we need to remember the name of Mrs. Doasyouwouldbedoneby, one of the characters in Charles Kingsley's nineteenth century children's classic: *The Water Babies,* and to teach as Mrs. Doasyouwouldbedoneby would teach. Similarly it might be useful to memorize the Biblical verse Luke

6:31 and apply that to our teaching as well: "As ye would that men should do unto you, do ye also to them likewise." Our language arts programs might be then alive with successes, not failures, with purpose, not pointlessness, with substance, not shadow. These are my hopes and my dreams. Am I asking too much?

11A
RESPONSE TO BASALS

BOBBI FISHER

I had been teaching for twenty years, and hadn't used a basal for the past twelve.

During the question-and-answer session of a workshop I was giving, a teacher asked me, "Why don't you use basals and workbooks, and how did you get away from them?" I told her that I had been teaching for twenty years, and hadn't used a basal for the past twelve. At one time I did use basals, but in the early 1980s I started introducing literature instead of basal materials and found that the children became more enthusiastic about reading *and* learning to read. Soon they became so involved in their own writing that there was less time for workbooks and worksheets.

I stopped using basals for several reasons. They detracted from the childrens' engagement in reading and writing and fostered ability grouping, a practice that I found abusive to the self-esteem of every child and detrimental to creating a community of learners who care about each other. Basal materials did not conform to the reading development of the individual children, and hindered and impeded their ability to gain control over their reading.

But I also told her what was happening in my classroom. I told her about some of the readers in my first-grade class. I told her about the enthusiasm and learning that goes on when children are engaged in "real" books. I shared with her how I evaluate and support their literacy development. I showed her examples of the conventions of writing, spelling, and voice that develop through the children's writing. I told her about my school, where reading and writing are woven into the fabric of the curriculum, and about the self-esteem and learning that goes hand-in-hand when children aren't restricted by ability reading groups.

I told her about Jerry, who is still an emergent reader at the end of first grade, but is beginning to gain control over print. "He wouldn't be good enough for the low group," in a basal classroom, but in my class he draws fabulous pictures, writes random letters and some beginning sounds, and participates enthusiastically during shared reading. I know that my first goal for him has to be "to make him look good" so he can join the community of readers and writers. I know he doesn't have a chance, and I don't have a chance with him either, if he doesn't feel he is a worthwhile member of the class.

I told her about Allison, who wrote a letter the first day of school telling me that she is interested in Egypt and the Revolutionary War. "She would have been too good for the top group," but in my class she reads lots of fiction and nonfiction and has gone through several chapter book series. I know that my goal for her is to expand her reading horizons.

I told the inquiring teacher about shared reading, when I demonstrate and the children participate in an array of reading and writing experiences. I do a lot of explicit teaching during that time, always relating it to a whole text (poem, song, or book) within the context of the conditions of natural learning.

I told her about the 30 minutes of silent reading in my class every day. At the beginning of the year, most of the children looked at the pictures, but as the year has gone on they have begun reading more and more. They're learning to read by reading.

I told her what *I* do during that silent reading time. I read myself for the first ten minutes and then children read to me individually. I record the date, book, strategies, miscues, teaching opportunities, and other comments pertinent to their reading development. I'm able to read with each child about twice a week.

I told her about writing time, when the children choose their own topics. Some write a single piece most days and others write books. Sometimes they write alone, and other times they collaborate. They write more and read more during that time than they ever would with worksheets and workbooks. When I look at their work over time, I see their growth in writing conventions, spelling, and content. They are confident writers and always want to share their work.

I told her about the school in which I teach where children are continually taking books out of the library, and are very engaged in reading and writing workshops. The "textbooks" for social studies are tradebooks and artifacts. A curriculum study for each grade culminates in a festival: a chicken festival for kindergarten; Japan Day for first grade; a Mexican fiesta for grade two; a Greek festival for third grade; and a Viking celebration for grade four.

Finally, I told her about the self-esteem of all the kids. It's high. There are no ability groups, just readers. There are no basals, just books.

11B
RESPONSE TO BASALS

BOB PETERSON

At La Escuela Fratney, we still believe that the best recipe for teaching reading is to hold the basal. Despite modest changes in the content of basal readers over the past several years—and huge changes in their packaging and advertising—there is no substitute for quality books. We believe this to be true not only in our reading program, but in our social studies and science programs as well.

So instead of shelves lined with identical copies of basal readers, our library and its closets are stuffed with book sets (averaging fifteen copies each). Because we are a two-way bilingual school we have sets in two languages: over 125 different ones in English and nearly 80 in Spanish. The sets include poetry anthologies like *Honey I Love* by Eloise Greenfield, science books like *The Magic School Bus. . .* by Joanna Cole, social studies books like Julius Lester's *To Be a Slave,* and dozens of children's novels. Each set is assigned a grade level, which means teachers at that grade level or above can use the books. This is so that teachers at the upper grades are assured that certain book sets haven't been read by their students in earlier grades. Each grade level has assigned book sets that are at a wide range of reading levels to accommodate the wide range of reading levels that the children bring into the classroom. As teachers develop materials for a particular book they (usually) put a copy with the set for future teacher use. In addition to the sets, we have over 140 big books in both English and Spanish with accompanying sets of small books to be used in our four- and five-year-old kindergartens and first and second grades. Such an operation requires considerable planning, support, and maintenance. Parent volunteers cover every paperback book with contact paper, and repair and replacement of lost items takes place on an annual basis.

But the benefits are well worth the effort. Two years ago, after a soon-to-be graduating group of Fratney fifth graders visited a feeder middle school, the librarian at the middle school library called to tell a Fratney staff member that he had been amazed at what he had seen when the Fratney students entered the library. "They went right to the shelves and started looking at the books," he recounted. "They were talking about books!"

In many ways finding appropriate texts for the school's reading program is easy compared to locating useful texts in the areas of social studies, science, and math. Many elementary teachers, burdened with overcrowded classrooms, virtually no planning time, and a multitude of subjects to prepare for, end up using textbook series in the subject areas as the foundation of their curriculum. Such a text-driven approach is beset with problems—from its lack of connection to student lives, to the over emphasis on "facts" that students are expected to absorb; from the

silencing of voices of groups of people who are outside the mainstream of society, to a style of writing
that produces high levels of boredom.

At our school teachers are beginning to use big
books and book sets that were originally purchased
for our reading program for social studies, science,
and math. New purchases of book sets are focused
on serving our multiple subject area needs. In these
lean times, however, a school's budget can buy only
so many book sets. Teachers need to use and develop
other reading resources as well. For example, in my
fifth-grade classrooms each student has a three-ring
binder to build our own "people's textbook." Using
binder dividers, we have sections for poetry, songs,
short stories, geography, current events, and different theme areas that we are studying. This allows our
class to draw on a variety of resources and to keep
them organized for ongoing classroom use. By the
end of the year my fifth graders will have an impres-
sive collection of poetry, song lyrics, and stories that
they can keep.

But regardless of whether textbooks or tradebooks
are used, teachers should help students reflect on
why they think the way they do; to realize that what
they have before them in their textbooks, in newspapers, or on the television is not always true. In other
words, to know that knowledge is "socially" constructed, that truth is relative not only to time and
place, but to class, race, and gender interests as well.
We engage our students in thinking about the validity
of their "texts;" in fact, this is one of the few uses I
have found for textbooks in my classroom. Students
can make good use of their textbooks by analyzing
why certain facts aren't included (for example, that
George Washington and Thomas Jefferson owned
slaves, that small pox-infected blankets were pur-
posely given to Native Americans, that Columbus
started the brutal trans-Atlantic slave trade, and so

Teachers need to use and develop other reading resources.

on). Students can also analyze whose voices are and whose voices are not being heard in stories and texts.

On a more subtle level, many texts use the passive verb tense to obscure reality. For example, in the most widely used elementary social studies text, the passive tense is frequently used to mask who was responsible for certain social conditions, such as the horrible working conditions found throughout much of our nation's history. The statement, for example, "there was little concern about worker safety" hides the fact that it was profit-hungry capitalists who showed little concern, and implies that the working people were apathetic. In fact, many people were "concerned," which led to organizing, lobbying, and militant strikes—none of which are mentioned in the text.

Helping students question the accuracy of textbooks and basal readers, or finding quality alternatives to such books, assumes, of course, that teachers have background knowledge about the subject area and have access to other sources of information. Books such as Howard Zinn's *A People's History of the United States*, are a good place for a teacher to start. It will be a sure way to spice up one's understanding of what has happened in our nation's past, and will help teachers as they try to create reading programs that speak to the needs of our children as they enter the twenty-first century.

11C
RESPONSE TO BASALS

SANDRA LAWING

Point Them to a Star
The children, with hands clasped,
  line the corridors of my memory.
I cannot, try as I may,
  extinguish their questioning surveillance.
Each child at some time stood close enough
  for me to reach and touch.
One, whose eyes are blue and endless,
  harbors the key to an elusive cure;
Another, who is pale and sad,
  possesses the insight to halt a future war;
A third—easily the most familiar—
  walks with the ancient poets and storytellers.
The rest, standing firm and resolute,
  clutch secrets to their bosoms.
Each, with pleading stares,
  has reached to me for wings and magic carpets;
Each, with open minds and hearts,
  begged me to point them to a star.

I think it is important to note that when I left the basal nine years ago, I didn't see it as an enemy.

Instead, as is so often the case,
    I turned the page and did what came next.
And, because of that singular impurity,
    heads shake hopelessly,
        bullets echo,
            and a rhyme dies unheard.

                                    Eugene V. Gallelli

I was once like Eugene Gallelli, author of the poem, "Point Them to a Star." For ten years I turned the page and did what came next and "as a result of that singular impurity," the basal very easily and quietly and under false pretenses became an enemy. I put my children's learning and their chance to become book-loving autonomous learners at risk by trusting people who did not know geographically *where* we were, much less *who* we were as readers and learners. Needless to say, I also put my professionalism in jeopardy.

I think it is important to note that when I left the basal nine years ago, I didn't see it as an enemy. I wasn't giving it up because I felt something was inherently wrong with it. I had never heard the term "whole language." I had done no professional reading on the major research that was being done and had already been done on literacy development. Neither had I visited classrooms where literature was being used. I had no knowledge of the reading process or of how children learn to read. My only background in reading was from teaching a basal program. My sole reason for leaving the basal was to give my children opportunities to read real books. Despite the basal's strangling and controlling hold and in spite of my fear of the unknown, something deep down inside of me knew that reading real books had to be better.

It was only after I left the basal that I realized how the stilted, unnatural language, the isolated skills, and the lack of choice were frustrating for children. I now know that basals rob children of real experiences with real language and authentic texts. They are too narrowly focused on the "subject" of reading as opposed to the more global picture of language development. They are confining, controlling, far too comfortable, and therefore, a big hindrance and obstacle to the development of teachers' growth, learning, and empowerment. Basals control our freedom as teachers to choose, thereby keeping us dependent on them as technicians—not as professionals. For years they prevented me from seeing the real world of reading as I graded children's reading on how well worksheets were filled in rather than assessing them on how well strategies were used to interact with and interpret a text. I documented children as they progressed through a *program*—not as they progressed as readers of real books. I never questioned why they didn't want to read and never enjoyed reading. I couldn't respond to what they were trying to do as readers because I lacked the necessary knowledge of reading and language development. I put my trust and time in a commercial, inanimate, temporary—we got new programs every five years—resource rather than trusting and investing in a real, living, lasting resource—*me*. Turning the page and doing what came next gave me no opportunities to invest in myself as a teacher and learner.

"But," say the publishers of basals who want us to think of them as experts on reading and children, "the basals are so much better now. We have anthologies of real literature—no adaptations, no controlled vocabulary. We have good illustrations, etc., etc." I have reviewed the "new and improved" basals. No matter how "good" the new ones are, no matter how well publishers succeed in using the jargon they think teachers want to hear, the fact remains that a commercially packaged, "quick fix" program controls our options as teachers and therefore as professionals. Any and all commercial programs limit our decisions and choices as teachers and children in dealing with our own individual interests, languages, cultures, and reading development.

In the years since leaving the basal, I have found that using authentic texts and giving children choices are powerful and necessary conditions in the development of children's learning, thinking, and autonomy. Basals fail to provide these conditions. An authentic text is not one among many in an anthology. An authentic text is one we can check out of a library or go to a bookstore and buy. In the real world outside the classroom, bookstores and libraries don't stock basals. Reading even the "best, new and improved" basal is not the same as reading a *real* book!

I began working with real books and away from basals nine years ago. I was teaching third grade and had to attend a mandatory workshop on *another* reading program. This workshop was to be different, though, because it was suppose to use *real* books. I entered that workshop with a closed mind and bad attitude. I was tired of the "powers that be" jumping on every educational bandwagon that came along and making me take the ride with them. Sure I wanted kids to read real books, but at that point saw no place or time for them in the existing reading program. Why, some days we were still doing reading groups after lunch!! When was there time for reading real books? Literature stayed on the shelves while the basal was done. I trusted the basal I was using to make readers of my children. (Actually I was naive and ignorant enough to think that I was the one trying to make readers of my children.)

Looking back on this workshop, I can see that it was very dated even then. No language theories were discussed. Nothing was said about how children learn to read. It was just another arbitrary grasp in the dark. Still, the program encouraged the use of real books and some writing—though both very teacher-directed. I decided to give it a chance.

It took only three weeks for the empowerment to begin for me and for most of the children. It was at this point that I began to see the basal as an enemy—one whose grip would be hard to break. I was having a hard time working away from some powerful mind-sets—ability grouping, isolated skills, the safety of being controlled. Adding to my own frustration was the frustration of two third-grade boys. They had been reading in pre-primers and were finding it difficult to make any connections with the literature books. They did not see themselves as readers. We would spend an hour with real books and they would still ask, "When are we going to read?" Their definition of reading was the comfort of a group, reading a rehearsed page, and doing worksheets. I couldn't rely on my knowledge of reading for help. I had none. I knew I had to do whatever was necessary to help those two boys develop some of the confidence and success the other children were feeling. We didn't give up. Time, patience, and determination helped those boys become confident, though not proficient readers, and by the end of the year they were reading Judy Blume and Beverly Cleary. Most importantly, they loved to read and saw themselves as readers—something the basal had failed to do for them.

During the last nine years, my lack of knowledge has often made me feel helpless, confused, and frustrated. Fortunately, I work in a school where teachers have opportunities to change, grow, and make decisions. I have had principals who trusted and treated me as a professional, peers who respected my decisions even if they didn't agree with them, and support and help from friends, fellow teachers, and family. I have had the benefit of two of the most knowledgeable people on children and literacy—Norma Kimzey of our regional North Carolina department of education and Lester Laminack of Western Carolina University. Yet despite all of this excellent support and knowledge, the journey from the safety and comfort

The journey from the safety and comfort of a commercial program to a more meaningful, realistic learning environment has not been easy.

of a commercial program to a more meaningful, realistic learning environment has not been easy. It has often been very scary—the criticism from some parents, my struggle for answers—but not once have I had any doubts about the decision to rid my classroom of all commercial programs. It is my responsibility as a professional to know as much as I can about my chosen work, to stay abreast and informed by reading professionally, networking, and attending conferences. I am the decision maker in my classroom. I find the answers for myself that support my belief in how children learn. I no longer want to be a victim because of circumstance or ignorance. It feels much better to be a proud, knowledgeable professional.

Books are the backbone of my classroom now. Children are constantly involved and immersed in print. Their reading is meaningful, relevant, purposeful, and abundant. They read more now in a day than they ever read in a month of basals. They have choices of which books they read and freedom to read alone, with partners, or in self-made groups anytime they want. They use books to research topics for their projects, to find answers to their questions, and for pleasure. They are comfortable and confident and unintimidated with any print. If something is too difficult, they don't say, "I can't." They say, "Will you help me?" Their autonomy has grown to the point where we now run classroom businesses, a café, a bank, a florist. This year we are adding a greeting card business. The children plan their day based on their decisions and my suggestions and assignments. Not surprisingly, none of this happened in the ten years I used the basals. All of this has happened as a result of getting out of commercial programs, exposing children to real experiences, and giving them choices that would empower them as learners, and hopefully prevent them from becoming victims.

I want to share a story that illustrates the importance of helping children become autonomous learners. She was a second grader who had been retained in first grade, but still had the determination and will to learn. She had already made a complicated spider project and presented her information in a game format. She did her research on spiders in rough draft form and took it through all of the steps of publishing until she had a beautiful, polished game board. She even wrote directions on how to play the game. As the children played the game, they answered questions about spiders. If they answered the questions correctly, they received a certain number of flies in their webs. The "spider" with the most flies in its web was the winner. She was also participating in a literature study over several days on *The Velveteen Rabbit*. One little boy was confused about why the rabbit had been taken away. A couple of children felt that the story was about love. She took my breath away when she said, "This story is about belonging. The rabbit belonged with the real rabbits. That is where he was supposed to be." She is a bi-racial child. I don't know if her comment had anything to do with being bi-racial, but as an empowered learner she helped me realize the power literature and choice can have on our learning, thinking, language, and lives.

And like the Velveteen Rabbit, our children belong with real experiences and real books. Our children deserve the best. The best doesn't happen by turning the page and doing what comes next, not if we want to be victors instead of victims.

11D
RESPONSE TO BASALS

KATHY MASON

The classroom was humming with the sounds of literate voices. Several children were reading poetry to each other from *The Dream Keeper* by Langston Hughes. A small group was creating a text set of all the books in the classroom that featured mice. (A few mice had made some unwelcome visits to our classroom over the summer. Mice are now a favorite subject in Room 126.) Another group of children were researching the Native American tribe they were interested in. As Tatum and I were sharing Jean Little's *Hey World, Here I Am,* I noticed a small group sitting on the floor by the basal texts that have been gathering dust under our chart board since August. Though these are brand-new adopted texts that according to district policy must be in plain sight in our classrooms, no one had ever noticed them before. I decided to observe this group from a distance. The children each

Luke had read the original and he found the story as it appears in the basal to be surprisingly inferior.

had a copy of the book opened to the same page and were choral reading. I watched and wondered: what were they discovering?

Little by little, we began to form our morning circle on the floor. In our multi-age, primary classroom, morning circle is called Life Circle. There are two reasons for this name. One is that Life Circle is one of the primary times during the day when we deal with events and issues that are crucial to the life of our classroom community. Another is we always bring our Life Books to that circle. Our Life Books are writers' notebooks (Calkins, 1991) in which we write our wonderings and our small noticings, inside and out. In addition to bringing these Life Books to Life Circle, we frequently bring the book we are reading or some piece of writing by an author whom we are studying at the moment.

That morning, Luke, the spokesperson for the small basal group, was very eager to share his feelings. Carefully and judiciously, he began his critical analysis, opening his copy of the basal to the story by Cynthia Rylant, *"The Relatives Came."* Luke had read the original and he found the story as it appears in the basal to be surprisingly inferior. "I get a different feeling when I read this book. It's not so poetic as the last time I read it." Lars added, "Remember yesterday, when we were talking about Thoreau and you said he wrote in the roots and not just on the branches? Well, this leaves you on the branches. It doesn't go into the roots. It's only surface, not below. They need real authors who know writing."

I began writing as fast as I could to get down the children's exact words. Several children, realizing the importance of this talk, urged, "Get the tape recorder!" But unfortunately, we had no audiotapes that day. So Britt and a few others joined me in writing down the talk in their Life Books. The following quoted speech, then, comes from their notes as well as mine.

Luke was warming to his topic, and Lars' metaphor sparked him as well as others.

> Luke: It didn't charge my batteries. It was like I had a dead battery after reading it. When your switch is turned on, it can get you into poetic places.
> Rob: Yeah, like *Peter and the North Wind*. This is not real literature. *Peter and the North Wind* is real.
> Luke: They shouldn't change literature. If the kids want to read this, they should get Rylant's real book. This is ordinary! I don't feel the setting. I don't get into the story. This is not literature.

Later, Luke added, "The clay remembers the hand that made it," a line from a book by Byrd Baylor. And still later:

> Luke: I feel embarrassed by this company—that they're doing this to books. They're turning it into junk. This book doesn't tell the whole story. It tells nothing. It's details only.
> Lars: They came; they did; they left.
> Rob: We're more of an author than they are.
> Luke (pointing to the teacher's edition): This book is like one big flashcard.

As our Life Circle was coming to a close, the children asked to see all of the basals that were behind my desk on the floor. They also noticed the spiral teacher's editions and asked to see those. I read a small portion to them. They were incredulous. "Why do they tell you what to ask us?" "How much did all of this cost?" "Do they pay for you to get books for our classroom?" "We need to talk with them (the basal publishers). When are they coming to Gilbert?"

Analyzing and critiquing the district's newly adopted "literature-rich" basal series has become a large-scale research project for the small group of children who originally began looking closely at the books. Luke, Lars, Spencer, Jeff C., and Britt in particular are checking out the original pieces of children's literature from our school library to compare with the basal versions. They are also going to invite the publisher's representatives to visit our classroom when they visit the district in December.

The basal investigation has spilled over into other parts of the day. Luke said he needed to put his mystery piece aside during writing workshop to write a letter to Scott, a term of address he later decided was too informal and which he changed to Mr. Foresman.

Luke voiced some concern about his position as an author. He asked if publishers always ask the author if they may change the original piece. He said he would read the contract very carefully when one is presented to him. He insisted he would not sign if his words are changed.

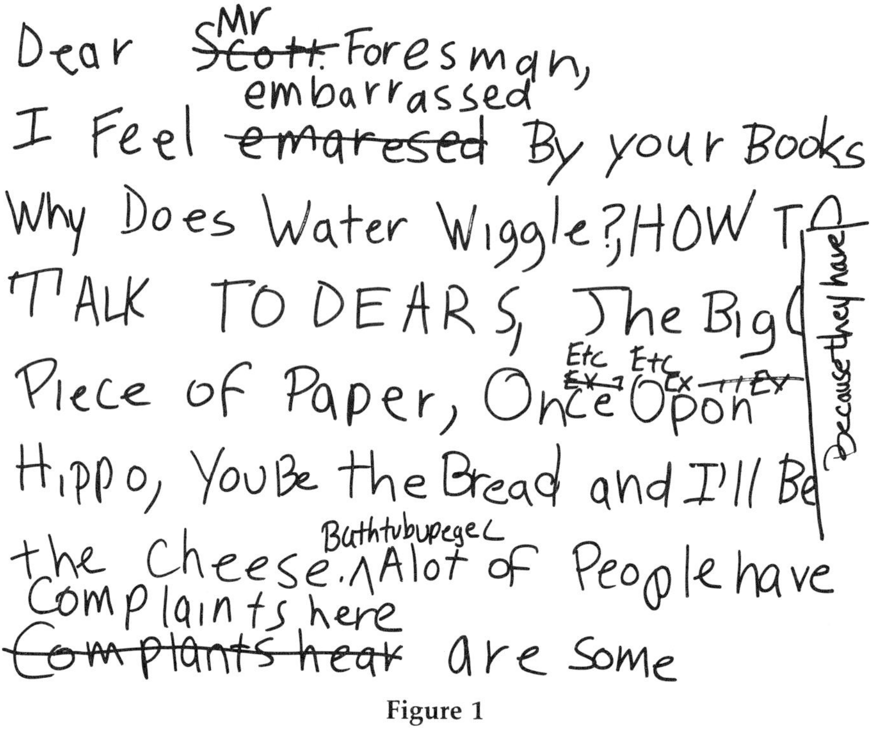

Dear ~~Scott~~ Mr. Foresman,
I Feel ~~emaresed~~ embarrassed By your Books
Why Does Water Wiggle? HOW To
TALK TO DEARS, The Big (because they have)
Piece of Paper, Once Opon Etc Etc Ex Ex Ex
Hippo, You Be the Bread and I'll Be
the Cheese. ∧Bathtubupegel Alot of People have
Complaints here
~~Complants heak~~ are Some

Figure 1

The Book you give the ~~teacers~~ teachers
~~These Big B~~ are Like one Big
flash Card. I Do not Like
your Comp. Becase your
trowing away poetic ~~lagwige~~ language
I Know what ~~Litcher~~ literature is and
this is not ~~Litcher~~ literature. The Books
~~heur~~ here are Just Books not ~~Litcher~~ literatur.
Kids reading your Books think
there reading Lit cher literature But there
~~not~~ ~~those Books are dctime~~ Please
~~Ploes~~ ~~Clouse~~ Close your comp or get
a real writer.
        Sined
            Luke D. Zeller

Figure 1 *(continued)*

Our classroom community has begun to wonder why established authors ever sign these contracts. Some children have decided it is for the money; others think it might be for getting a wider audience. In the meantime, I am once again, aware—and grateful—that I spend my days with truly literate people.

12

SUPERVISING CHANGE: MOVING AWAY FROM BASALS

TIMOTHY J. SHANNON

Alarming new research on illiteracy in America indicates that without a profound change in direction, most American school children will not become lifelong readers—that one of four will scarcely learn to read at all. We launched the California Reading Initiative in May 1986 in response to this frightening problem, and the equally startling realization that 40 percent of those Americans who can read books choose not to. The goal of the Initiative is to turn this disastrous trend around by encouraging students to develop lifelong positive attitudes towards reading and stimulating educators to change and improve their reading programs. (Honig, 1988, p.235)

My school district received a document entitled *Recommended Readings in Literature, Kindergarten Through Grade Eight* from the California Department of Educa-

The Initiative called for movement beyond the basals to reading programs that promoted the use of multicultural, multilingual children's literature.

tion in March, 1986. It listed 1,010 "good books" selected for use in restructuring the reading programs of California school districts. This document was the beginning of "a comprehensive plan to revitalize the teaching of reading and the language arts through curriculum and resource development" (Honig, 1988, p.236). The California Reading Initiative promised not only literature suggestions, but an *English/Language Arts Framework for California Public Schools, K-12* that "sets the stage for bringing this new and integrated 'whole language' approach to the classroom" (Honig, 1988, p.239). Beginning with statements about research on present reading programs, the Initiative caused administrators to think about the basal reading programs in their schools. Excellent teachers had known for many years that change in reading programs must come. The Initiative called for movement beyond the basals to reading programs that promoted the use of multicultural, multilingual children's literature. The document stated that the use of literature would improve attitudes toward reading in that the learners would be given a choice in what they read and what they learn.

Clearly, the intent of the Initiative was to use literature in its original form as the basis for reading instruction. The literature-based program would bring teachers and learners out of the lockstep movement through the story-questions-workbook format of the basal reader to a classroom full of students and teachers enjoying the reading of good books. The framework provided by the Initiative would give teachers suggestions of how to accomplish this goal.

The state provided each district with copies of the framework late in the 1986–1987 school year. Telephone calls ensued among district superintendents about the structure and spirit of the documents. The general feeling at the time was to wait and see what was to follow. The state had a reputation for sending initiatives frequently and not backing them up with clear timelines or funds for implementation. Questions were also raised about the intent of the state in issuing this initiative. Was it a mandate? Top-down reading initiatives in the past usually connoted mistrust. They implied that the state believed districts could not improve reading programs on their own. Typically, directives tightly tied districts, teachers, and students to set procedures, materials, or tests. The initiative, however, had taken away one of the tools of mistrust in advocating the movement beyond basals, but it failed to ameliorate a second by providing an assessment tool that could properly assess new types of reading programs.

I had learned early from my colleagues not to be too quick to express an opinion about an issue that was sure to be controversial.

When the Framework arrived, I found myself having nearly completed my second year as a teaching/principal/superintendent of a small one-school district in northern California. The document sounded good, but I had learned early from my colleagues not to be too quick to express an opinion about an issue that was sure to be controversial. I needed help in determining a course of action for the ensuing school year and brought the Initiative up in the final staff meeting of 1986–1987.

Our staff meetings usually took the form of a discussion. After our immediate concerns were out of the way, we would usually end the meetings with a "show and tell" time when staff would bring up things that they wanted to share or things that concerned them about the school, their job, or the community. I introduced the Initiative and asked the teaching staff for help in determining what was known and what was unknown about this new directive. The teachers immediately raised some interesting questions about the implementation of the Initiative: What is the timeline for implementation of the new program? What are some of the things that the state is doing to help teachers make the changes in the classroom? What do parents think about the possibility of the change positively affecting students' reading and interest in reading? And finally and most importantly, who will evaluate the program and what methods of evaluation will be used? I used these questions to direct my efforts before we proceeded any further.

WHAT IS THE TIMELINE FOR IMPLEMENTATION OF THE NEW PROGRAM?

I informally consulted my colleagues during the next county superintendents' meeting. Many stated that they were not going to move swiftly on this issue because there was no timeline and no reason to rush into implementation until there was an established timeline. Some commented that in their districts the sentiment was generally supporting the basal reading series in the present form. The administrations were concerned that the community still felt that the basals were more than adequate to teach reading to their children and that it was the teachers who were to blame for the students' poor performances on the standardized reading tests. The teachers were just not working hard enough using the basal readers to improve test scores. By and large, most administrators adopted a "wait and see" position on the implementation of the Initiative, afraid in some cases to talk about any specific timelines for change. Until a timeline was provided, there would be no hurry.

WHAT ARE SOME OF THE THINGS THAT THE STATE IS DOING TO HELP TEACHERS MAKE THE CHANGES IN THE CLASSROOM?

Most administrators, myself included, had previously been inundated with new programs without the funding or the technical support needed to put them in place. The Initiative seemed to be another case in which the state suggested or mandated a new program without the funding to back it up. If the basal reader was to be abandoned, then there had to be funds to purchase other books for the students to read. The state reimbursement, however, was still only allocated for textbooks, and basals were considered textbooks, while tradebooks or children's books were not. No provisions had been made for buying the new books that children were now supposed to read.

Many teachers were comfortable using the basals, and building principals were unsure if these teachers could be "retrained."

Moreover, many teachers were comfortable using the basals, and building principals were unsure if these teachers could be "retrained" to deliver a quality reading program without them. At this point, certain administrators doubted that the tenured "poor" teachers of their district would be able to wean themselves off the structured basals and use any alternative methods. Without more specific state guidelines or funds for in-service, administrators felt that the district would have to design entirely new reading curriculum by themselves.

A county-wide effort on the part of teachers produced teacher-prepared guidelines on many of the books listed in the *Recommended Readings in Literature, Kindergarten Through Grade Eight*. The teacher guides were stored in the county resource center so that a teacher who chose to use the alternative teaching methods could obtain copies of questions, activities, and tests to supplement the book they used. These stop-gap measures were funded by the county to get something ready for the teachers to use during the coming school year. School boards were amazed at how quickly the teachers, working throughout the summer, could prepare the amount of material that became available in the resource center.

Many district offices selected stories and books from the literature list to develop specific curriculum for each grade level. Then, for example, a third-grade teacher could merely look at the teacher-prepared curriculum guide for her grade level, arrange to obtain the books used by her district, and go to the resource center and copy the questions, activities, and tests that had been prepared for those books. Many teachers who were given the freedom to choose the literature for their classroom made choices of books based on the quality and quantity of the teacher-prepared materials.

WHAT DO PARENTS THINK ABOUT THE POSSIBILITY OF THE CHANGE POSITIVELY AFFECTING THE STUDENTS' READING AND THEIR INTEREST IN READING?

In my district, the parents were usually willing to go along with what the school suggested. They felt that the school had their children's best interest in mind. The teachers were well respected in the community and were thought to be doing a good job. The possible movement away from basals was generally accepted once it was explained thoroughly and carefully during special parent meetings. Our problems arose from parents who did not attend the meetings and who were against the elimination of any textbooks from the classroom. They had been educated with basal readers and were not about to entertain the idea of allowing their children to choose the books that they would read and what they would learn. After all, that was the teacher's job.

Parent opinion of the Initiative was the topic during many lunches when district administrators from the county got together. Horror stories were swapped, ranging from parents who protested the movement away from basals to teachers who would complain to the parents and then support them in an effort to keep basals in the classrooms. Most school systems continued to use the California Test of Basic Skills, of which the reading portion contained reading skills aligned very closely with the skills taught in the basal readers.

At times, teachers would tell parents that they were concerned about their children's test scores, fearing that the scores would drop if the Initiative were fully implemented. These teachers cited the similarity between tests and basals as their reason for their fear. Because the public newspapers, the media, and many parents rated school districts and teachers according to scores on reading tests, many administrators feared that the Initiative would depress test scores and cause panic in their districts.

The state did not change their evaluation procedures at all.

WHO WILL EVALUATE THE PROGRAM AND WHAT METHODS OF EVALUATION WILL BE USED?

The state left the evaluation of the success of the Initiative to the school districts. They were to set goals and to determine the degree to which those goals were met. The State of California would still evaluate the school with the California Assessment Program (CAP) tests. The CAP tests were administered to the third, sixth, and eighth grades in all school districts in order to assess each school's curricula. The state did not change their evaluation procedures at all. Despite the requests for radically different reading curricula, "Reading assessment is still based on multiple-choice questions in California . . ." (Honig, 1988, p. 238). Moreover, the CAP tests were rumored to be linked to state funding, the primary source of funding for school districts. Higher scores would mean higher funding; lower scores would mean lower funding, growth plans, and possible takeovers. This rumor put increased pressure on the district, which in turn increased pressure on the principals and the teachers to keep their basals and stabilize their CAP scores. The teachers became increasingly frightened for their students, their jobs, and their communities.

It was my feeling that all educational eyes were on

the State of California and all those California educators who believed that the move beyond the basal reader was a good one. The teachers who were already teaching with alternative methods or who were interested in trying to eliminate the basal were now not as excited about the California Reading Initiative.

OUR NEW PROGRAM

At the beginning of the 1987–1988 school year, our teachers got together before the students returned to discuss the Initiative and what was to be done about it in the upcoming year. I addressed the questions that the teachers had asked in June and asked the teachers if they felt comfortable with implementing the Initiative. The responses that I received were positive on the general theme of the Initiative, but teachers still needed reassurance that there would be few, if any, negative repercussions if they were to begin another round of risk-taking with a new curriculum. It was my job to minimize the pressures of a new program on teachers who were willing to try the alternative reading approach, and to promote the program in every way possible with the community and the school board. It also became my job to develop an evaluative system for the new program that would reflect accurately the students' progress and be easily related to parents and the school board. The latter was difficult because the school district was obligated to administer the California Assessment Program (CAP) tests and was still testing student achievement with the California Test of Basic Skills (CTBS). Neither test accurately reflected the learning that was to take place in the classrooms. While teachers were aware of this mismatch, the school board and the parents were not. We decided to go ahead with the alternative reading program and hold parent meetings to inform them of the progress and the setbacks of the new reading program. We decided:

1. The classroom teachers would develop a time-line for implementing the goals of the Initiative.
2. The teachers would begin by supplementing the basals with teacher-prepared activities. They would then move away from basals into literature of the classroom community's choosing.
3. The district would develop an alternative evaluation method to reflect the goals of the Initiative. Our evaluation plan was to hold individual parent conferences and show the parents what students were actually doing in class and how they liked reading and writing more under the new program.

Basal anthologies are still in the school to this day. However, they are used only by one primary teacher. She explains that she uses them to create feeling of confidence among kindergartners who can read a whole story with the controlled vocabulary of the basal. "The basals," she explains, "will never be re-purchased." She spends her book money to buy children's books instead.

OTHER DISTRICTS LOOK BACK

I called other principals and superintendents in California to listen to their recollections about the Initiative and the movement away from basals. Other districts in northern California met with much more resistance in moving beyond basals. Some superintendents recognized the ineffectiveness of the basal much earlier than the May 1986 Reading Initiative. They categorized teachers into two camps—those who religiously used the basals page-by-page and those who supplemented the basals with enrichment activities of their own creation. The former group, comprised predominantly of veteran

In many cases, teachers were competing with each other to finish their grade level readers.

teachers, greatly outnumbered the latter. Superintendents recounted that they heard discussions in the teachers' lounge about which story teachers were on or the fear that they would not make it through the book by the end of the year. In many cases, teachers were competing with each other to finish their grade level readers. Supervisors found that students were bored with reading class. For the most part, the children were reading stories that they did not want to read, "learning" skills that they already knew, and slugging through workbooks to get on to the next story. Some students were competitive enough that they gained pleasure from simply getting through the stories quickly and competed with the others to be finished faster.

These superintendents were relieved to see the Initiative come along because now they had the authority to demand change from all teachers. They went right to work with the implementation of the alternative ways to teach reading. They held meetings to inform teachers of the Initiative and sought opinions on the use of literature without basal texts. They sent their teachers to workshops to learn how to teach without basals. They organized teacher groups, who prepared sets of questions and activities and stored them where all teachers could use them. They were concerned with state testing not aligning itself with the reading programs suggested in the Initiative and sought to develop improved evaluation methods to assess the progress under the new programs. However, teachers were slow to convert, and some did not convert at all. Parents organized to help get the school system "back to basics" by putting pressure on the school board to do something about "improving their children's education."

These district superintendents believed in the new alternative methods and took the heat from their communities, holding seemingly endless meetings to inform the parents about the advantages of the new programs. What changed parents' minds about basals and tests were their children, who began to share books that they had read in school with their parents. They talked about plays that they had written to dramatize a story that they had read in class. After only one year, the children in the alternative classes were excited about reading, parental concern began to subside, and administrators began to feel justified in their stand against the basal.

Of course, many problems remained. Foremost among these was how to justify the reading programs with evaluation systems that the parents and the school boards would understand and accept. Each district had to independently work through these problems. During my interviews with several California superintendents and principals, one explained, "[Our evaluation systems] had to reflect progress and not merely increased interest in reading." Test scores dipped initially and did not improve significantly until four years later. One superintendent stated, "I hate to admit it, but the state must have done something right. We would never have made a move so positive had it not been for the California Reading Initiative. The district presently has a whole language program in grades K–3, and a literature-based reading program in grades 4–8. The high school has recently begun using a writing program that pushes writing across the curriculum." When asked what his literature-based program looked like, he replied, "we use the Macmillan literature program." He was very happy to report that the CAP tests were now using performance-based assessment in science and social studies and that the language arts portion would soon become performance-based. He felt comfortable that the CAP tests had been changed sufficiently to reflect the learning and teaching in the classrooms.

The California Reading Initiative offered an opportunity to progressive teachers. It provided research

Fear of declining test scores delayed the full implementation of a much needed change.

and policy to support teacher's movement beyond basals, which had previously caused the teacher dependence on lockstep methods of teaching reading. The Initiative also provided a large list of "good books" that stimulated student interest in reading. It was well written and flexible enough to allow districts to choose the timeline for implementation, and left the degree of usage to schools. It implied that the State trusted school districts to make changes, and it encouraged teachers to take risks in designing their own curriculum. However, the Initiative failed to anticipate the resistance from parents and teachers, the "retraining" required, or the problems districts would have in implementing a new program without an assessment tool that could reflect the learning and teaching that was to go on in classrooms. Fear of declining test scores delayed the full implementation of a much needed change that would facilitate learning. On one hand, the Initiative implied trust by removing basals, but on the other hand, it failed to trust districts and teachers enough to stop the constant testing.

SUPERVISING CHANGE

> . . . It seems that every three years, someone—whether it's a new hotshot superintendent, the state department, the governor, or a university professor—comes up with some great new idea of how American education is to be saved. What happens is that my colleagues and I become the punching bag recipients of someone else's plan.
>
> Why is it so hard for people outside the classroom, including you folks from the university, to understand that we teachers know at least as much about our students, teaching, and ways to improve as you do! (Glickman, 1989, p. 5)

The sentiments of Sam, as recounted by Carl Glickman, reflect the frustrations of professionals throughout the field of education. They wonder why so few "outsiders" trust them. At one time in my own teaching career, I closed the door, put down the basal, and began teaching in a manner conducive to building interest, and in turn building a learning environment. I had tried other methods—I let the learners choose the topics because that was what I thought my job was. In this sense, the California Reading Initiative was not invented by the State Education Department, but rather it was brought about by like-minded professionals who finally opened their classroom doors, demanded trust, and (after sensing a receptive State Superintendent) began writing change at the state, district, and school levels.

Whatever success the Initiative may enjoy in California is due to those at the bottom as well as those at the top. Many suggest that change must come from the bottom up—from teachers and learners (Weaver & Henke, 1992; Glickman, 1990; Sergiovanni, 1987; Garman, 1988). Although these writers alluded to trust, they have not made it a central focus of school change or supervision literature. I think this is a mistake. Trust is the essential component in all lasting reforms, and it must pervade schools from the bottom up and the top down. Without trust in its many forms, schools can only change in superficial ways. First, teachers must trust themselves. This is not as easy as it sounds within the traditional authority structures of schooling with all the trappings of simple, bureaucratic, and technical control. Carl Glickman suggests, "The banner word of the restructuring movement is *empowerment*, and it places the school at the center of inquiry, raising questions about the conventional structures of schooling" (1990, p. 69). Without top-down directives, teachers must ask questions and seek answers for themselves. They must take risks and accept responsibility for the failures as well as successes of changes in curriculum and teaching. This requires a simple trust among professionals who will

Trust in the classroom must be established early.

strive to do the right thing based on practical and theoretical knowledge. This self-trust that coincides with the democratic ideals of shared governance is long lasting and builds the professionalism, intellectualism, and sagacity needed to adopt and carry out change programs that work.

A second form of trust is among the learners, parents, and classroom teachers. This trust requires changes in the authority structures of classrooms. Learners and their parents must believe that the teacher in their classroom is there for one purpose only—to help children learn. This trust is often of an intangible, wavering variety brought about by teachers collaborating with parents and learners to design programs built on choice, time, and responsibility. Trust in the classroom must be established early because it correlates highly with students' risk taking, interest, and learning.

A third form of trust is among administrators at all levels, and the teachers in their districts.

> Many of the teachers saw trust between principal and teachers as revolving around the opportunity to disagree without fear of reprisal. In other words, trust between principal and teachers meant respect for the job each does in the school. As one teacher stated, "I want to know that he appreciates the fact that I am a good teacher and can make good decisions (Short, Greer, & Michael, 1991, p. 135).

This desire to be appreciated as a professional reflects the climate that must be established within districts to bring about any school reform. Teachers need the trust of administrators to create long-lasting change in their classrooms and this requires change in the authority structures at district and state levels.

If real change is to take place in reading programs and schools, districts and state officials can no longer define success as mere compliance with central office or state level programs: reform movements cannot come every three years; no more sweeping paradigm shifts; no prodding of teachers to adopt a new top-down policy by the not-so-subtle leverage applied through accountability schemes. Statements like, "We're doing whole language," "We use such and such a basal," or "We have a literature-based program" will not be necessary. Instead it will be sufficient for superintendents, principals, and supervisors to report: "I trust that our teachers are doing what is best for the learners of this district."

13

THE SOCIAL LIFE OF BASALS

PATRICK SHANNON

*Since the
inception of
basals during the
1920s, advocates
have tried to deny
that basals have
social lives.*

People are not the only ones with social lives.
Things have them also; that is, when those things
come into contact with people. From Calvin's Hobbes
to Stephen King's Christine, authors have exploited
this social life for many years. But things do not need
to take on anthropomorphic characteristics to have a
social life. Just their existence within a particular context has social consequences—some good, some bad.
Consider what the invention of the automobile has
meant to our lives. We have the ability to travel great
distances rapidly and the freedom over time to travel,
but the roads to carry those cars have dissected our
communities and the exhaust has fouled our air. Not
only do things have social lives, but those lives are
complex.

Since the inception of basals during the 1920s, advocates have tried to deny that basals have social lives.

They argue that "basals are only things," and they propose strict separation between discussions of these things and their use. This putative separation is, at once, impossible and self-serving. First, basals were and are published with the intent that they will be used. Moreover, current editions of basals are developed based on a history of their social life; that is, how they have been used in elementary school classrooms—at times as window props, but more often as regimen for all activities during reading lessons. For publishers and advocates to deny this social life is to negate their basic justification for the continuation of some of the more objectionable parts of basals (*e.g.*, workbooks, skills tests, and so on) because they claim that teachers desire these basal parts for what they do during reading lessons. For if it were not for the social life of these basal parts, publishers could produce basals in completely different forms with each new edition.

Second, advocates' denials of the social life of basals attempt to absolve publishers and themselves of all responsibility for the consequences of basal use and abuse. I think this denial is fundamentally wrong. People are morally responsible for the social life of the things we develop, build, or advocate because we intend and know that they will be used. Advocates and basal reading series do not have an exemption from this ethic, and advocates must take responsibility for the purpose for which basals are put together, the ways in which they are assembled, the manner in which they are sold, educators' intents for their use, and all the impacts basals have on teachers' and children's lives in elementary schools, and later, in life. As my mother says, "In for a penny, in for a pound" (which of course is quite apt, given the sums of money involved in this business). If advocates hope to change basals' social life, then they must radically alter the historical and social relationships embedded within them. However, as this book and the *Report*

Card on Basal Readers suggest, and basal advocate Dolores Durkin (1987) confirms, basals have not really changed at all.

NEW EDITIONS

To avert continued criticism, basal advocates ask "are the examples from basal materials and the descriptions of their development that are used to argue for how they deskill teachers representative of current materials or publishing practices?" (Baumann, 1992, p. 394). The truth about the social life of basals belies this "the new edition took care of that" defense. Disregard the fact that such statements acknowledge that past criticism has been accurate, and consider that the market that demands a new edition every five years or so also demands that the new editions stay pretty close to their predecessors. Basal publishers, advocates, and many teacher educators have created this market for basals over the last 60 years by promising that basals will deliver predictable standard results regardless of the school environment. They make the same claim with each new edition. To radically alter the form of basals would be to undermine publishers' credibility with their market concerning the comprehensive nature of previous editions. For if publishers were inaccurate with their earlier claims, why should consumers trust them now?

Because each basal publisher makes the same claim and they make it for each new edition, there is very little difference in form among the different series or editions. Content may vary, the order of skills may vary, certainly the rhetoric can vary, but the teacher's manual still spells out which skills are to be taught, when, and toward what level of mastery. All this "advice" is offered in the imperative. Over the years, basal form has only become more sophisticated, more complete, more totalizing in its explicitness.

Modest changes are necessary with each edition.

Of course, modest changes are necessary with each edition, if basals in general and publishers in particular want to retain their share of the market. To distinguish themselves from their competitors and from their own preceding editions, basal publishers sell more and more ancillary materials to apparently insatiable consumers. Rather than offering real choices to teachers and students, these additional materials intensify reading lessons, giving more and more work for teachers and students to do in less time. Some 1993 basal series have three teacher's manuals to cover what they call "level one" alone. Moreover, if basal publishers did not change the content of some instructional materials and directives, they would lose their illusion of cutting-edge pedagogy and science (Chall, 1983), and if they did not change the surface structure of biases, they would lose their claims of multicultural relevance and fail to meet state adoption mandates (Marshall, 1991). Let me be more explicit about why these alterations are not real changes.

The most prevalent rationale offered to use the new editions of basals is that the new anthologies put good literature in the hands of American children (in many cases for the first time) and that this is a cause for celebration. Although I do not dispute the judgment that the literature in the basals is good, I am unconvinced that they put this literature in children's hands. The literature that basals offer children is still in the control of others—teachers, publishers, and basal advocates. Both the literature and the children, as readers of that literature, are subjected to the same constraints as the stories in previous basal editions.

One of our son Tim Pat's favorite authors, Miriam Cohen, has allowed Scott Foresman to reprint *It's George* in the 1993 edition of *Celebrate Reading* (Level 1E, pp. 104–133). The story is situated in a basal lesson with the traditional Directed Reading and Thinking Activity (DRTA) format. Students are made ready for the text by being given vocabulary, a purpose, and some leading questions. The story is divided into parts, and at the end of each part, readers' interpretations of the story are directed by questions. At the story's end, readers are given a comprehension check that asks them to pretend they are George and draw and write a letter telling a friend what they did. The teacher's manual for the story "guides" the teacher to "accept" drawings that show what George did. Answers will vary but should include the following: "Dear _____, I went to visit my friend. He fell off his chair. I could not get him up, so I called 911 to get help. I saved my friend's life. George."

To me, this is not putting good literature in children's hands. Rather, it is using good literature to practice the same skills and strategies that have driven reading instruction in schools for the last 60 years. When Tim Pat, his sister Laura, or other children choose to read Miriam Cohen's books about friendship and life in primary grades, they do not do a DRTA and they do not develop such a narrow understanding of her stories. Good literature has a more profound impact when it is not reduced to a practice text. While basalized literature has previously been easy to identify as the clipping of words and illustrations from original tradebooks, I think now we must acknowledge that the basalization of literature is also a narrowing of the potential for good literature to make a real impact in the lives of young readers. I do not mean to imply thought control here; certainly teachers and students can disregard the teacher's manual and simply read the anthologies. However, the regimen toward literature in the new editions may well lead those students who do not do well on the skills that surround the stories to hate both reading and literature. Previously, when children were asked about their literacy, many replied that they hated reading, but they read all the time. What this typically meant was that they often read books, magazines, cereal boxes, advertisements, and other printed mate-

Advocates also offer multiculturalism as a reason to use the new editions of basals.

rial, but they disliked reading lessons at school. I worry now that good literature will be similarly tainted.

Advocates also offer multiculturalism as a reason to use the new editions of basals. They argue that basal publishers have made a commitment to multiculturalism that is often found lacking among tradebook publishers. This rationale can only refer to an economy of scale, and not to a commitment to diversity, because most of the basal stories were previously published as tradebooks. Basals provide a significant number of multicultural stories through their anthologies at a much lower cost per unit than tradebook publishers make available in single editions. However, when advocates offer this rationale they rarely mention this economic consideration (I'm certain the sales staff don't miss any opportunity to make this point, though); rather, they imply that those who teach from the new editions are prepared to build a kinder and gentler nation.

I do not mean to make light of the need for children to find themselves in the stories they read in and out of schools or of the possibility that multicultural literature can expand readers' understanding of others. But I do question the celebration of basal publishers' recent commitment to multiculturalism and the behaviorist belief that mandated multicultural literature will change intolerant attitudes, actions, and structures in schools.

Basal publishers' commitment to multiculturalism has a decidedly economic tinge of another sort. When California, a single textbook adoption state, finally put teeth in their demand that all textbooks treat multiculturalism seriously, basal publishers hired multicultural authors, advisors, and consultants and started including good multicultural literature in their anthologies. Before that time, their commitment seemed dubious at best. Most basals chased multiculturalism rhetorically, coloring the faces of the human characters or switching to anthropomorphized animals in their texts. I do not doubt the sincerity and good intentions of the people involved in the development of the new editions, but I question deeply the corporate commitment to multiculturalism beyond the marketplace.

Moreover, I worry about the behaviorist logic that drives this whole approach to multiculturalism. California demands and basal advocates hope for multicultural literature because they expect literature to be the appropriate stimulus to evoke tolerant behavior and understanding among teachers and students within a system built, and still based on, racism, classism, sexism, homophobia, and religious, ethnocentric, and language biases. This may sound harsh, but multiculturalism is as much about power as it is about understanding, and the new editions of basals do little to change the power structure even in reading lessons. They still include a single scope and sequence of skills that privilege white, middle- and upper-class males. They still test through standardized procedures. They still promote grouping by ability. While multicultural literature has some potential to foster and support understanding, mandating it within schools and classrooms where multiculturalism is unappreciated will not make this a kinder, gentler nation. The California Department of Education and basal advocates should know that opinions and private behaviors can not be legislated—even when they happen in a public domain.

If basal publishers are truly committed to multiculturalism, perhaps they will commit some of their profits to initiate concentrated, serious, multicultural inservice programs within the districts that adopt their basals. When publishers send in their facilitators, they should bring along their anthologies to allow teachers to discuss the good literature among themselves so that they do not have to follow the narrow interpretations suggested in the teacher's manual.

By 1990, there were six corporations that controlled over 90 percent of the market.

MONOPOLISTIC COMPETITION

The elementary school reading market is so lucrative (over $400,000,000 a year) that mergers, buyouts, and takeovers have significantly reduced the competition among basals, redistributing the market shares among corporations and making it more difficult for innovation to break through. During the 1930s, there were over 100 basals available. When I started to write about basals in 1981, there were fifteen competing publishers. By 1990, there were six corporations that controlled over 90 percent of the market. Macmillan/McGraw-Hill (which owns Merrill, SRA, and Barnell Loft), Harcourt, Brace, Jovanovich (which owns Holt, Rinehart), Silver Burdett-Ginn (which bares its merger in its title), Houghton Mifflin, Scott Foresman, and D.C. Heath. (During the summer of 1993, Harcourt, Brace, Jovanovich made a bid to buy Macmillan/McGraw-Hill.) This movement toward oligopoly makes it very difficult and risky for companies to venture into this market because each new edition costs in excess of $20 million just to allow the newcomer to compete for only ten percent of the market. The potential return cannot justify this considerable investment. Moreover, the concentration of control makes for some strange bedfellows in the basal market. For example, Macmillan/McGraw-Hill publishes two basals, Distar, SRA kits, and the *Whole Language Catalog* and its supplement. Can't you just see the sales staff talking to prospective customers? "You want basals? We publish two (four if the buyout happens)! You want scripted phonic lessons? We got 'em. And whole language assessment? Fine, we do that, too!" Under no circumstances can advocates of basals say that the corporations that own basals take a principled stand on how children learn to be literate. It's money that matters.

The corporations that publish basals also publish tests to demonstrate that their programs can certify that students are learning to read. Several state education departments require that basal publishers produce such documentation before they allow publishers to market their goods to districts in those states. Some of these corporations publish standardized, norm-referenced reading achievement tests as well. In 1990, Macmillan/McGraw-Hill published the California Achievement Test, the California Test of Basic Skills, and the SRA Achievement Test; Harcourt, Brace, Jovanovich published the Metropolitan Achievement Test and the Standard Achievement Test (if the 1993 buyout happens Harcourt, Brace, Jovanovich would own five leading achievement tests); and a subsidiary of Houghton Mifflin produces the Iowa Test of Basic Skills.

It is not by coincidence that the basals of these corporations use the same testing formats, vocabulary, and skills as are found on the standardized tests they produce. The Lake Wobegon Effect (*i.e.*, all children are above average in Lake Wobegon) is achieved when school districts apply basal materials, take the appropriate standardized test, and then compare their test results with a norming group who never saw the basal or test vocabulary, formats, or skills before. This, of course, is a marketer's dream because beleaguered administrators who are forced to define the success of their reading programs by test scores must find it compelling to listen to sales personnel guarantee not only high criterion-referenced test scores, but high norm-referenced test scores as well. This is what is called a vertical oligopoly in the business world—one set of corporations controls prices and production at two levels of the same market.

Because, as the authors of the essays in this book attest, all basals are basically alike, publishers are faced with the same problem as automobile makers when all cars look alike. Accordingly, the few corporations still in this market spend high percentages of their budgets to advertise the incidentals of basals that

In a way, the new editions of basals are just like the new models of automobiles each year.

make their products appear distinct from their competitors. Anyone who has attended the International Reading Association or the National Council of Teachers of English annual conventions knows about the advertising campaigns that substitute for in-depth analyses of learners' and teachers' needs beyond consumption or differences among products. This example of monopolistic competition didn't just happen by chance. The new social life of basals among multinational corporations made it not only possible, but also necessary, because the bottom line in accounting ledgers makes the decisions.

In a way, the new editions of basals are just like the new models of automobiles each year. The forms remain the same (although we have the knowledge and technology to do it differently), but they look and feel much better. Even with this knowledge of the gimmickry of new models, we cannot disassociate ourselves from the social life of automobiles because our lives are now organized to drive for our living. Most of us cannot conceive of a life without our cars because we could not find food, work, or clothing nearby. Because of the ways that teachers' and students' lives are set up at school and the ways they are prepared for that life, many administrators, teachers, and parents can't conceive of reading instruction without basals. Basals and texts are not just things, as their advocates maintain, they play a major part in the everyday life of schooling.

CONSEQUENCES FOR STUDENTS

Although at first it might seem odd, school lessons and basal readers do not teach anyone to read. People learn to be literate on their own, commensurate with the demands for written communication in their immediate environments. Sometimes these demands are social; sometimes they are personal; but most often they are a combination of the two. People are successful in developing sophisticated literacies by themselves because they have access to environments that demand sophisticated literacies. Their instruction at school has or had an impact on their literacy development, but often not in the way we've been taught to think about it. Rather than teaching people to read and write in a sophisticated manner, school lessons—both explicit and tacit—teach some people that they have a right to be in those environments, and that once there, they are relatively likely to be successful. Other people learn at school that they do not belong in environments that demand sophisticated literacies and that they will fail if given the opportunity.

Without apology, schools are designed to sort students according to ability, in order that society will benefit from the best and the brightest filling the most demanding roles. In fact, almost all of schooling is structured explicitly toward this end (*e.g.*, grade levels, ability grouping, testing, marking, and so on), but even most school procedures sort students implicitly (*e.g.*, who is called on to answer, what classroom responsibilities are given to whom, and where students sit in approximation to the teacher, among other situations). Schools are designed to deliver a meritocracy, and basals are organized to facilitate this design.

However, as Shirley Brice Heath (1983), Gordon Wells (1985), David Bloome (1987), and others have demonstrated through years of field work, the structures and procedures of schooling in general and literacy lessons in particular are not meritocratic at all. Rather they are culturally determined and biased in favor of white, middle- and upper-class, male students from nursery to post secondary school. That is, the sorting at school—explicit and implicit tracking—takes place along gender, racial, and social class lines. Those tracks present different opportunities and inculcate different subjectivities among the various social groups according to their expected social

Basals and their advocates do nothing to prevent social biases from directing the processes and outcomes of schooling.

function. Both teachers' expectations and students' aspirations are directly influenced.

Although basal readers do not teach anyone to read, they do provide a scale for sorting students by so-called "language abilities." With their narrow scope and sequence of skills, basals supply the yardstick with which to gauge students. Basals' predetermined paths cut along racial, gender, and social class lines (Luke, 1988; Bloome & Nieto, 1987) and provide the technical means to fulfill the biased prophecies of who are winners and who are losers in the race to do well at school as a preliminary heat for the race for employment. With the illusion of scientific certainty and with the backing from business, many university professors, and the state, basals legitimize schools' and society's biased sorting. Since all students are apparently measured against the same scales, basals often blind students and their parents to the fact that social groups are systematically treated differently during school reading lessons, preparing some for better futures than others. In the same way, basals shield teachers from recognizing their duplicity in the perpetuation of the unjust social *status quo* in the United States.

Of course, basals don't cause the sorting, but to steal a phrase from Jo Fraatz (1988), they "mobilize bias." That is, basals and their advocates do nothing to prevent social biases from directing the processes and outcomes of schooling. The rich get richer while the poor get poorer. Basals play a central role in overcoming the apparent contradictions between the meritocratic rhetoric that surrounds American schools and the unequal access to prestigious environments and literacies.

DESKILLING OF TEACHERS REVISITED

Because of the "new edition will cure all" mentality, advocates of basals live only in the present or the soon-to-be present with each new edition. Since "new" automatically connotes progress in America, basal advocates believe that they do not have to accept responsibility for these past injustices to students or to teachers. Looked at historically, with each new edition, more and more of the teaching responsibilities have been moved to higher levels of school and publishing bureaucracies. This process of subtraction has been justified through economic, scientific, and psychological grounds. First, removing the responsibilities for teaching from teachers means that one standard can be used across the school, district, state, and country. Second, as new "scientific" discoveries are made they can be delivered to teachers and students technically, through the materials. Third, those standard materials will evoke a standard response from teachers and ensure a standard student product. In the *Report Card on Basal Readers,* we discussed this issue as the commodification of reading instruction and the deskilling of teachers. The critique behind these concepts has caused fits among basal advocates, because it cuts deeply into the mystique that surrounds basals and requires the elimination of basals in any attempt to improve literacy programs in schools. Both have been the central focus of written responses from basal advocates (*e.g.,* Allington, 1993; Baumann, 1992; Squires, 1987). I'd like to reaffirm, and perhaps clarify, our position on these issues.

Commodification means that reading instruction has become a thing to sell. Perhaps this is no more apparent than the *Hooked on Phonics* advertisements on radio and television. As a commodity, reading instruction is packaged and tailored to markets as much as any other product. Even advocates admit as much. "Publishers rely heavily on research to produce their curricula, but it is market research that more often carries the day—not basic research" (Allington, 1992). The human activity embedded in commodities is secondary to its salability. This is what happens with

New editions or not, basals commodify reading instruction.

basals, wherein authors and consultants become interchangeable parts and components of programs are developed and assembled separately with in-house editors making major decisions about text, lesson plans, practice activities, and testing according to their market research.

While technologically sophisticated, market research is really quite simple. Its purpose is to gage the market for a particular product by posing questions and situations that create the need for a particular product. Despite basal advocates' recent attempts to bring respectability to such research (*e.g.*, Allington, 1993), basal market research is not at all an open-ended investigation of what administrators, teachers, and students think about reading and reading instruction, and it is *all* about studying already-convinced administrators and teachers in order to find out how to sell more products to that market. In this way, market research is a closed circuit that can't deny the need for basals, and the market (not teachers and students) make decisions about what will happen during reading instruction.

In a sense, basal authors and consultants are like Michael Jordan and his various lines of clothing. No doubt Mr. Jordan and basal authors consult with manufacturers about their respective commodities, but basals authors are no more the writers (creators) of basals than Michael Jordan is the designer of his clothes. It doesn't matter that he wears few designs from his collection during his everyday life; his name sells the product, just like basal "authors' " names sell basals. Some basal authors may even publicly question the value of their products in a way similar to Cybil Shepard's remarks that she doesn't like to dye her hair. But L'Oréal® keeps her in the public eye just the same, because despite her concerns, she sells their products to people who see her name and head, but do not hear or pay any attention to her complaints. New editions or not, basals commodify reading in-

struction, and even reading itself, through their connections with standardized reading achievement
tests.

At first, basals were simply a collected or created
set of reading materials with a few suggestions for
teachers that were included in the anthologies themselves. According to Venezky (1987), early basal publishers worried that teachers would reject even these
modest suggestions because of their intrusion into
teachers' responsibilities. However, with each new
edition, a few more of the teaching tasks (setting
goals, planning lessons, deciding how and when to
test, and so on) were absorbed by the basals and encoded into the teacher's manual, basal tests, and other
paraphernalia. This historical process is what we
mean by the concept of the deskilling of teachers. We
do not mean, as Baumann (1992) and others carica-
ture, that basals are used as pliers, in the way old-
fashioned dentists use them, to extract skills from
teachers. Rather, teachers' responsibilities, defini-
tions, and practices of their job have changed qualita-
tively over time, just as other workers', as the technology of their work has expanded its social life (Banta,
1993). More and more of the decision-making and
planning skills are ceded to management and beyond,
until workers become appendages to the technology.
This is not a conspiracy theory, but a recognized fact.

> Teacher education programs are often designed as if
> teachers were responsible for establishing appropriate
> educational objectives for their students, preparing
> appropriate curriculum materials, conducting and
> evaluating the outcomes of instruction, and making
> whatever adjustments should prove necessary in
> these activities. Teachers may have done all these
> things in the past, but at present, most of these
> functions are performed by school boards, school ad-
> ministrators, and commercial publishers (Brophy,
> 1982, p. 11).

If anyone is questioning teachers' intellect, it's basal publishers.

Such statements could not be made accurately about other professions—law, engineering, or medicine—which have taken control of the technology of their respective professions and made it subordinate to their own authority. In reading lessons, however, the role of technology and human beings have reversed so that the latter works for the former. This is not a critique of teachers' intellect as basal advocates have charged (Allington, 1993; Baumann, 1992). Rather, deskilling is a historical process that is a natural outcome of the commercialization of any activity. We are simply reporting research on the social life of basals. Are Allington and Baumann and other basal advocates questioning teachers' intellect when they report their findings from their research on how teachers should think and act in different ways than they think and act now? If anyone is questioning teachers' intellect, it's basal publishers, who feel the need to script lessons in the teacher's manual because apparently they believe teachers would not know what to do without someone putting words in their mouths, goals in their heads, and all the materials they need in their hands.

In fact, we have spent much of our time since the *Report Card on Basal Readers* finding and writing about teachers of the past and present who for one reason or another questioned the commercialization of reading instruction and have neutralized or fought off the deskilling of teachers (*e.g.*, Bird, Goodman, & Goodman, 1991, 1992; Shannon 1990, 1992). Most, if not all of them, have not used basal materials and have been successful in helping people learn to read in sophisticated ways. We applaud their actions and find that more and more teachers are trying to forge a different social life for basals, one that has basals all dressed up every five years or so, but with no place to go.

REFERENCES

Aardema, V. 1981. *Bringing the Rain to Kapiti Plain.* New York: The Dial Press.

Allington, R. 1993. "Letter to the Editors: Reply to Shannon." *Reading Research Quarterly* 28: 216.

Allington, R. 1992. Personal Communication.

Altwerger, B., and Resta, V. 1986. "Comparing Standardized Test Scores and Miscues." Paper presented at the annual meeting of the International Reading Association, Philadelphia, PA.

Alvermann, D., et al. 1993a. *Heath Reading: A Program Overview.* Lexington, MA: D.C. Heath and Company.

Alvermann, D., et al. 1993b. *Heath Reading. Rare as Hen's Teeth: Teacher's Edition.* Lexington, MA: D.C. Heath and Company.

Alvermann, D., et al. 1993c. *Heath Reading. Rare as Hen's Teeth: Think and Write Workbook.* Lexington, MA: D.C. Heath and Company.

Alvermann, D., et al. 1991. *A Guide to Journal Writing.* Lexington, MA: D.C. Heath and Company.

Alvermann, D., et al. 1991a. *Little Duck Dance.* Lexington, MA: D.C. Heath and Company.

Alvermann, D., *et al*. 1991b. *A Soft Pillow for an Armadillo*. Lexington, MA: D.C. Heath and Company.

Alvermann, D., *et al*. 1989, 1991a. *Heath Reading: My Best Bear Hug*. Lexington, MA: D.C. Heath and Company.

Alvermann, D., *et al*. 1989, 1991b. *Heath Reading: Never a Worm This Long*. Lexington, MA: D.C. Heath and Company.

Alvermann, D., *et al*. 1989, 1991c. *Heath Reading: Rare as Hen's Teeth*. Lexington, MA: D.C. Heath and Company.

Alvermann, D., *et al*. 1989/1991. *Heath Reading: (Gr. 1,3,5 tests)*. Lexington, MA: D.C. Heath and Company.

Aoki, E.M., *et al*. 1993a. *A New View. Staff Development Magazine*. Macmillan/McGraw-Hill.

Aoki, E.M., *et al*. 1993b. *A New View. A to EZ Handbook: Staff Development Guide*. Macmillan/McGraw-Hill.

Aoki, E.M., *et al*. 1993c. *A New View. Writer's Workshop: Handbook for Reading/Language Arts Teachers*. Macmillan/McGraw-Hill.

Aoki, E.M., *et al*. 1993d. *A New View. Catch a Sunflake: Teacher's Planning Guide*. Macmillan/McGraw-Hill.

Aoki, E.M., *et al*. 1993e. *A New View. Catch a Sunflake: Literature Activity Book*. Macmillan/McGraw-Hill.

Apple, M.W. 1986. *Teachers and Texts: A Political Economy of Class and Gender*. New York: Routledge.

Ardizzone, E. 1980. "Creation of a Picture Book." In *Only Connect: Readings on Children's Literature*, 2nd ed., edited by S. Egoff, G.T. Stubbs, and L.F. Ashley, 289–298. Toronto/New York: Oxford University Press.

Arnold, V., and Smith, C. 1990a. *Reading Express: In the Wild*. New York: Macmillan Publishing Company.

Arnold, V., and Smith, C. 1990b. *Reading Express: On the Track*. New York: Macmillan Publishing Company.

Arnold, V., and Smith, C. 1990c. *Reading Express: Orbits*. New York: Macmillan Publishing Company.

Arnold, V., and Smith, C. 1990c. *Reading Express: Bold Dreams*. New York: Macmillan Publishing Company.

Asch, F. 1981. *Just Like Daddy*. New York: Simon & Schuster.

Ashbrenner, B. 1986. *Children of the Maya: A Guatemalan Odyssey*. New York: Dodd.

Associated Press. 1993. "Minorities Now a Majority in Many U.S. Areas." *Arizona Daily Star*, 9 June.

Atwell, N. 1987. *In the Middle*. Portsmouth, NH: Heinemann.

Austin, M., and Morrison, C. 1963. *The First R*. New York: Wiley.

Banta, M. 1993. *Taylored Lives: Narrative Productions in the*

Age of Taylor, Veblen, and Ford. Chicago, IL: University of Chicago Press.

Barrera, R., Liguori, O., and Salas, L. 1992. "Ideas a Literature Can Grow On: Key Insights for Enriching and Expanding Children's Literature About the Mexican-American Experience." In *Teaching Multicultural Literature in Grades K–8,* edited by V. Harris. Norwood, MA: Christopher-Gordon Publishers.

Barrett, J. 1970. *Animals Should Definitely Not Wear Clothing.* New York: Atheneum.

Barringer, F. 1993. "Foreign-Speaking U.S. Residents Increase by 38.1 Percent in '80s." Fresno, CA: A1,A6.

Barton, A., and Wilder, D. 1964. "Research and Practice in the Teaching of Reading." In *Innovations in Education,* edited by M. Miles. New York: Teachers College Press.

Baumann, J.F., et al. 1993a. *New Dimensions in the World of Reading: Making a Wish* (Teacher's Edition). Needham, MA: Silver Burdett-Ginn.

Baumann, J.F., et al. 1993b. *New Dimensions in the World of Reading: On the Horizon* (Teacher's Edition). Needham, MA: Silver Burdett-Ginn.

Baumann, J.F., et al. 1993c. *New Dimensions in the World of Reading: On the Horizon: Reader's/Writer's Notebook.* Needham, MA: Silver Burdett-Ginn.

Baumann, J.F., 1992. "Basal Reading Programs and the Deskilling of Teachers: A Critical Examination of the Argument." *Reading Research Quarterly* 27: 390–398.

Bird, L.B., ed. 1989. *Becoming a Whole Language School: The Fair Oaks Story.* Katonah, NY: Richard C. Owen.

Bishop Sims, R. 1982. *Shadow & Substance: Afro-American Experience in Contemporary Children's Fiction.* Urbana, IL: National Council of Teachers of English.

Bishop, R. 1992a. "Multicultural Literature for Children: Making Informed Choices." In *Teaching Multicultural Literature in Grades K–8,* edited by V. Harris. Norwood, MA: Christopher-Gordon Publishers.

Bishop, R. 1992b. "Recent Trends and Issues in Children's Books About People of Color." Presented at the Research in Language and Literacy Weekend Series: Literacy Research Informs Teaching/Literacy Teaching Informs Research. Tucson, AZ: Department of Language, Reading and Culture, The University of Arizona, December 4 & 5.

Black, H. 1967. *The American Schoolbook.* New York: Morrow.

Black, J., and Martin, R. 1982. "Children's Concepts About Writing at Home and at School." Paper presented at annual meeting of the National Council of Teachers of English, Washington, DC.

Bloome, D., and Bailey, F. 1990. "From Linguistics and Education, a Direction for the Study of Language and Literacy: Events, Particularity, Intertextuality, History, Material, and Dialectics." Paper presented at the National Conference on Research in English, Chicago, IL.

Bloome, D., ed. 1987. *Literacy and Schooling*. Norwood, NJ: Ablex.

Bloome, D. and Nieto, S. 1989. "Children's Understandings of Basal Readers." *Theory Into Practice* 28: 258–264.

Booth, D. 1984. "What Will I Wear?" In *Catch a Rainbow-Impressions*, general editor J. Booth, 4–10. Toronto, ON: Holt.

Booth, J., ed. 1984. *Impressions (Grade One)*. Toronto, ON: Holt.

Booth, J., coordinating author. 1985. *Impressions (Grade Three)*. Toronto, ON: Holt.

Booth, J., senior author. 1987/1988. *Impressions*. Toronto, ON: Holt.

Bridge, C.A., Winograd, P.N., and Haley, D. 1983. "Using Predictable Materials vs. Preprimers to Teach Beginning Sight Words." *Reading Teacher* 36 (9): 884–891.

Brophy, J. 1982. "How Teachers Influence What is Taught and Learned in Classrooms." *Elementary School Journal* 83: 1–13.

California Department of Education. 1991. *Recommended Readings in Spanish Literature: Kindergarten Through Grade Eight*. Sacramento, CA: Curriculum, Instruction and Assessment Division.

California Department of Education. 1992. Language Census Report for California Public Schools. Sacramento, CA.

Calkins, L. 1991. *Living Between the Lines*. Portsmouth, NH: Heinemann.

Calkins, L.M. 1986. *The Art of Teaching Writing*. Portsmouth, NH: Heinemann.

Cameron, I., and Mickelson, N. 1989. "Whole Language and Basal Readers." *Reflections on Canadian Literacy* 7: 267–271.

Chall, J. 1967. *Learning to Read: The Great Debate*. New York: McGraw-Hill.

Chall, J. 1983. *Learning to Read: The Great Debate*. 2nd ed. New York: McGraw-Hill.

Christian-Smith, L.K. 1989. "Power, Knowledge and Curriculum: Constructing Femininity in Adolescent Romance Novels." In *Language, Authority and Criticism*, edited by S. de Castell, A. Luke, and C. Luke. London: The Falmer Press.

Cianciolo, P. 1976. *Illustrations in Children's Books*. Dubuque, IA: William C. Brown Publishers.

Cole, J. *The Magic School Bus* series. Scholastic.

Cullinan, B.E. 1989. "The National Reading Initiative: Outgrowth of the California Reading Initiative." *The New Advocate* 2 (2): 105–113.

Cooney, B. 1982. *Miss Rumphius*. New York: Puffin Books.

Doyle, K., program editor. 1984. *Journeys*. Toronto, ON: Ginn.

Durkin, D. 1987. "Influences on Basal Reading Programs." *Elementary School Journal* 87: 331–341.

Durkin, D. 1981. "Reading Comprehension Instruction in Five Basal Reading Series." *Reading Research Quarterly* 16: 515–544.

Durr, W.K., *et al.* 1989a. *Houghton Mifflin Literary Readers, Book 1*. Boston, MA: Houghton Mifflin Company.

Durr, W.K., *et al.* 1989b. *Houghton Mifflin Literary Readers, Book 3*. Boston, MA: Houghton Mifflin Company.

Durr, W.K., *et al.* 1989c. *Houghton Mifflin Reading Language Arts Program K–8*. Boston, MA: Houghton Mifflin.

Duvoisin, R. 1980. "Children's Book Illustration: The Pleasures and Problems." In *Only Connect: Readings on Children's Literature*. 2nd ed., edited by S. Egoff, G.T. Stubbs, and L.F. Ashley, 299–316. Toronto/New York: Oxford University Press.

Edelsky, C. 1992. "A Talk with Carole Edelsky About Politics and Literacy." *Language Arts* 69: 324–329.

Edelsky, C. 1991. *With Literacy and Justice for All*. London: Falmer Press.

Edelsky, C. and Draper, K. 1989. "Reading/'Reading'; Writing/'Writing'; Text/'Text'." *Reading-Canada-Lecture* 7: 201–216.

Edelsky, C. and Smith, K. 1984. "Is That Writing—Or Are Those Marks Just a Figment of Your Curriculum?" *Language Arts* 61: 24–32.

Erickson, F. 1984. "School Literacy, Reasoning, and Civility: An Anthropologist's Perspective." *Review of Educational Research* 54: 525–546.

Farr, R. and Strickland, D., *et al.* 1993a. *Treasury of Literature: At My Window* (Teacher's Edition). New York, NY: Harcourt Brace Jovanovich, Inc.

Farr, R. and Strickland, D., *et al.* 1993b. *Treasury of Literature: A Friend Like You* (Teacher's Edition). New York, NY: Harcourt Brace Jovanovich, Inc.

Farr, R. and Strickland, D., *et al.* 1993c. *Treasury of Literature: Across the Fields* (Teacher's Edition). New York, NY: Harcourt Brace Jovanovich, Inc.

Farr, R. and Strickland, D., *et al.* 1993e. *Treasury of Literature: The Deep Blue Sea* (Teacher's Edition). New York, NY: Harcourt Brace Jovanovich, Inc.

Farr, R. and Strickland, D., *et al.* 1993f. *Treasury of Literature: Sliver of the Moon* (Teacher's Edition). New York, NY: Harcourt Brace Jovanovich, Inc.

Farr, R. and Strickland, D., *et al.* 1993g. *Treasury of Literature: Like a Thousand Diamonds* (Teacher's Edition). New York, NY: Harcourt Brace Jovanovich, Inc.

Farr, R. and Strickland, D., *et al.* 1993h. *Treasury of Literature: Light up the Sky* (Teacher's Edition). New York, NY: Harcourt Brace Jovanovich, Inc.

Fischer, R.M., *et al.* 1972. *Football*. London: Blackie and Son.

Fischer, R.M., *et al.* 1972. *Lost at Football*. London: Blackie and Son.

Fischer, R.M., *et al.* 1972. *Michael's Bump*. London: Blackie and Son.

Flood, J. and Lapp, D. 1990. "Types of Writings Included in Basal Reading Programs, Kindergarten Through Second Grade: An Investigation of Changes from 1983 to 1989." In *Literacy Theory and Research: Analyses from Multiple Paradigms. Thirty-Ninth Yearbook of the National Reading Conference*, edited by J. Zutell, S. McCormick, M. Connolly, and P. O'Keefe, 395–410. Chicago, IL: National Reading Conference.

Florio, S. and Clark, C. 1982. "The Functions of Writing in an Elementary Classroom." *Research in the Teaching of English* 16: 115–130.

Fox, M. 1993. *Time for Bed*. San Diego: Harcourt Brace and Co.

Fox, M. 1992. *Dear Mem Fox I Have Read All Your Books, Even the Pathetic Ones*. New York: Harcourt Brace Jovanovich.

Fox, M. 1986. *Zoo Looking*. Melbourne: Martin Educational.

Fox, M. 1986. *Wilfrid Gordon McDonald Partridge*. New York: Viking/Kestrel.

Fraatz, J. 1988. *The Politics of Reading*. New York, NY: Teachers College Press.

Freeman, D.E., and Freeman, Y.S. 1992. "Enriching Primary Language Print Resources." *CABE Newsletter* 15 (2): 9–20.

Freeman, D.E., and Freeman, Y.S. 1993. "Strategies for Promoting the Primary Languages of All Students." *The Reading Teacher* 46 (7): 552–558.

Freeman, Y. 1991. "Literature-Based or Literature: Where Do We Stand?" In *The Whole Language Catalog*, edited by K. Goodman, L. Bird, and Y. Goodman, 189. Santa Rosa, CA: American School Publishers.

Freeman, Y. 1989. "Literature-Based or Literature: Where Do We Stand?" *Teachers Networking: The Whole Language Newsletter* 9 (4): 13–15.

Freeman, Y.S. 1988. "The California Reading Initiative: Revolution or Merely Revision?" *The New Advocate* 1 (4): 241–249.

Freeman, Y.S. 1988a. "The Contemporary Spanish Basal Reader in the U.S.: How Does it Reflect Current Knowledge of the Reading Process?" *NABE Journal* 13 (1): 59–74.

Freeman, Y.S. 1988b. "Do Spanish Methods and Materials Reflect Current Understanding of the Reading Process?" *The Reading Teacher* 41 (7): 654–664.

Freeman, Y. 1988c. "Métodos de Lectura en Español: Reflejan Nuestro Conocimiento Actual del Proceso de Lectura?" *Lectura y Vida* 9 (3)s: 20–28.

Freeman, Y. 1987. "The Contemporary Spanish Basal in the United States." Doctoral dissertation, University of Arizona, Tucson.

Freeman, Y., and Cervantes, C. 1991. "Literature Books on Español for Whole Language Classrooms." In *Occasional Papers: Program in Language and Literacy*, edited by K. Goodman and Y. Goodman. Tucson, AZ: Office of Language and Literacy, University of Arizona.

Freeman, Y., and Goodman, Y. 1993. "Revaluing the Bilingual Learner Through a Literature Reading Program." *Reading and Writing Quarterly: Overcoming Learning Disabilities* 9: 163–182.

Galeano, E. 1988. "In Defense of the Word." In *The Graywolf Annual Five: Multicultural Literacy*, edited by R. Simonson and S. Walker, 113–126. St. Paul, MN: Graywolf Press.

Garman, N.B. 1988. "Teachers Ask: Is There Life After Madeline Hunter?" *Phi Delta Kappan* 69 (9): 669–672.

Gee, J. 1989. "What Do English Teachers Teach? (Or Why Isn't the Pope a Bachelor?)" *Journal of Education* 171: 135–147.

Gee, J. 1991. *Social Linguistics and Literacies*. London: Falmer Press.

Geertz, C. 1973. *The Interpretation of Cultures: Selected Essays*. New York: Basic Books.

Glickman, C.D. 1993. *Renewing America's Schools*. San Francisco, CA: Jossey-Bass Publishers.

Glickman, C.D. 1990. "Open Accountability for the '90s: Between the Pillars." *Educational Leadership* 47 (7): 38–42.

Glickman, C.D. 1990. "Pushing School Reform to a New Edge: The Seven Ironies of School Empowerment." *Phi Delta Kappan* 72 (1): 68–75.

Glickman, C.D. 1989. "Has Sam and Samantha's Time Come at Last?" *Educational Leadership* 46 (8): 4–9.

Glickman, C.D. 1984–1985. "The Supervisor's Challenge: Changing the Teacher's Work Environment." *Educational Leadership* 42 (4): 38–40.

Goffman, E. 1959. *The Presentation of Self in Everyday Life.* Garden City, NY: Doubleday Anchor Books.

Goldstone, B.P. 1989. "Visual Interpretation of Children's Books." *The Reading Teacher* 42 (8): 592–595.

Goodman, K.S. 1992. "I Didn't Found Whole Language." *The Reading Teacher* 46: 188–199.

Goodman, K.S., Goodman, Y., and Bird, L., eds. 1992. *The Whole Language Assessment Supplement.* New York, NY: American Book Publishers.

Goodman, K.S., Goodman, Y., and Bird, L., eds. 1991. *The Whole Language Catalog.* New York, NY: American Book Publishers.

Goodman, K.S., *et al.* 1988. *Report Card on Basal Readers.* Katonah, NY: Richard C. Owen.

Goodman, K.S., *et al.* 1987. *Language and Thinking in School.* 3rd ed. Katonah, NY: Richard C. Owen.

Goodman, K.S. 1987. *What's Whole in Whole Language?* Richmond Hill, ON: Scholastic.

Goodman, K.S. 1987. In *Reading Miscue Inventory: Alternative Procedures.* Katonah, NY: Richard C. Owen.

Goodman, K.S. 1986. *What's Whole in Whole Language?* Ontario, Canada: Scholastic.

Goodman, K.S. 1982. "Testing in Reading: A General Critique." In *Language and Literacy: The Selected Writings of Kenneth S. Goodman.* Vol. 2, *Reading, Language and the Classroom Teacher,* edited by F. Gollasch, 289–298. London: Routledge & Kegan Paul.

Goodman, K.S., 1982. "Miscue Analysis: Theory and Reality in Reading." In *Language and Literacy: The Selected Writings of Kenneth S. Goodman.* Vol. 1, *Process, Theory, Research,* edited by F.V. Gollash, 103–113. London: Routledge & Kegan Paul.

Goodman, K.S., and Page, W. 1978. *Reading Comprehension Programs: Theoretical Bases of Reading Comprehension Instruction in the Middle Grades.* Tucson, AZ: NIE.

Goodman, Y.M., Watson, D., and Burke, C. 1987. *Reading Miscue Inventory: Alternative Procedures.* Katonah, NY: Richard C. Owen.

Gordon, C.J. 1991. "English Language Arts Instruction and Assessment in Canada." *Reflections on Canadian Literacy* 9 (3 & 4): 153–158.

Grant, C., and Sleeter, C. 1989. "Race, Class, Gender, Exceptionality, and Educational Reform." In *Multicultural Education: Issues and Perspectives*, edited by J. Banks and M. Banks, 46–76. Boston, MA: Allyn & Bacon.

Graves, D.H. 1983. *Writing: Teachers and Children at Work.* Portsmouth, NH: Heinemann.

Halliday, M. 1985. *An Introduction to Functional Grammar.* Baltimore, MD: Edward Arnold.

Harman, S. 1991. "National Tests, National Standards, National Curriculum." *Language Arts* 68 (1): 49–50.

Harris, V. 1986. "The Brownies' Book: Challenge to the Selective Tradition in Children's Literature." Doctoral dissertation, University of Georgia, Athens.

Harste, J.C., Short, K.G., and Burke, C.B. 1988. *Creating Classrooms for Authors.* Portsmouth, NH: Heinemann.

Harste, J., Burke, C., and Woodward, V. 1982. "Children's Language and World: Initial Encounters with Print." *Final Report, NIE Project G-79-0132.* Washington, DC: National Institutes of Education.

Hayden, R. 1991. "An Evaluation of the Reading and Writing Components of Holistic Language Arts Series' Workbooks." *Reflections on Canadian Literacy* 9 (3 & 4): 139–146.

Heald-Taylor, G. 1991. *Changes.* Orlando, FL: Harcourt Brace Jovanovich.

Heald-Taylor, G. 1989a. *Imagination, An Odyssey Through Language: Changes.* San Diego, CA: Harcourt Brace Jovanovich.

Heald-Taylor, G. 1989b. *Imagination, An Odyssey Through Language: Wonders.* San Diego, CA: Harcourt Brace Jovanovich.

Heald-Taylor, G. 1989c. *Imagination, An Odyssey Through Language: Visions.* San Diego, CA: Harcourt Brace Jovanovich.

Heald-Taylor, G. 1987. "Predictable Literature Selections and Activities for Language Arts Instruction." *Reading Teacher* 40: 6–12.

Heard, G. 1989. *For the Good of the Earth and the Sun: Teaching Poetry.* Portsmouth, NH: Heinemann.

Heath, S.B. 1983. *Ways with Words.* New York, NY: Cambridge University Press.

Honig, B. 1988. "The California Reading Initiative." *The New Advocate* 1 (4): 235–240.

Hopkins, L.B. 1991. "'Leave Me Alone,' Cries the Poem." *Perspectives* 7 (3): xiii–xv.

Hopkins, L.B. 1987. *Pass the Poetry Please*. New York: Harper & Row.

Houston, J. 1972. *Songs of the Dream People*. New York: Atheneum.

Huck, C. 1976. *Children's Literature*. New York: Holt, Rinehart & Winston.

Hymes, D. 1970. "The Ethnography of Speaking." In *Readings in the Sociology of Language*, edited by J. Fishman, 99–138. The Hague: Mouton.

Ingram, A.B. 1987. *Making a Picture Book*. Melbourne: Methuen Australia.

Jeffers, S. 1991. *Brother Eagle, Sister Sky*. New York, NY: Dial Books.

Johnson, T., *et al*. 1987. "People Eat Sausages to Love: Evaluating a Grade One Reading Program." *Canadian Journal of English Language Arts* 10 (2): 44–50.

Kabagarama, D. 1993. *Breaking the Ice: A Guide to Understanding People From Other Cultures*. Boston, MA: Allyn & Bacon.

Keystone State Reading Association. 1992. Personal Communication. Champion, PA: Keystone State Reading Association 25th Annual Conference.

Kiefer, B. 1983. "The Responses of Children in a Combination First/Second Grade Classroom to Picture Books in a Variety of Artistic Styles." *Journal of Research and Development in Education* 16 (3): 14–20.

Klassen, C. 1993. "Teacher Education That is Multicultural: Expanding Preservice Teachers' Orientation Toward Learning Through Children's Literature." Doctoral dissertation. Tucson, AZ: Department of Language, Reading, and Culture, University of Arizona.

Krumgold, J. 1953. *. . . and Now Miguel*. New York, NY: Thomas Y. Crowell Company.

Lacy, L.E. 1986. *Art and Design in Children's Picture Books*. Chicago: American Library Association.

Laws, F. 1980. "Randolph Caldecott." In *Only Connect: Readings on Children's Literature*. 2nd ed, edited by S. Egoff, G. Stubbs, and L. Ashley, 317–325. Toronto/New York: Oxford University Press.

Leont'ev, A. 1978. *Activity, Consciousness, and Personality*. Englewood Cliffs, NJ: Prentice-Hall.

Lester, J. 1968. *To Be a Slave*. New York: Dial.

Lester, N.B. and Onore, C.S. 1990. *Learning Change*. Portsmouth, NH: Boynton/Cook Publishers.

Lorraine, W. 1980. "An Interview with Maurice Sendak." In *Only Connect: Readings on Children's Literature.* 2nd ed., edited by S. Egoff, G. Stubbs, and L. Ashley, 326–336. Toronto/New York: Oxford University Press.

Los Angeles Times. 9/29/93, page E1.

Luke, A. 1988. *Literacy, Textbooks, and Ideology.* Philadelphia, PA: Falmer.

MacLachlan, P. 1980. *Through Grandpa's Eyes.* New York: Harper & Row.

Malicky, G. 1990. "The What and Why of School Literacy." *Reflections on Canadian Literacy* 8: 136–138.

Manning. D.A., and Fennacy, J.W. 1993. "Bringing Children to Literacy Through Shared Reading." In *Bringing Children to Literacy: Classrooms at Work,* edited by B. Harp. Norwood, MA: Christopher-Gordon Publishers.

Marshall, D. 1991. "Publishers, Protesters, and Texas Textbook Decisions." In *The Politics of the Textbook,* edited by M.L. Apple and L. Christian-Smith. New York, NY: Routledge.

Martin, Bill. 1992. *Little One* series. New York: Holt, Rinehart, and Winston.

Martin, B. 1990. *Bill Martin's Sounds of Language.* Allen, TX: Developmental Learning Materials.

May, J.P. 1991. "Exploring Book Illustration as a Work of Art." *CLA Bulletin* (summer): 2–4.

Mayer, M. 1967. *A Boy, a Dog and a Frog.* New York: Dial Books.

McInnes, J. 1988. "In School Today." In *Across the Water—Networks.* Toronto, ON: Nelson.

McInnes, J., *et al.* 1983. *Networks (Grade Five).* Toronto, ON: Nelson.

McInnes, J. (1986/1987/1988). *Networks (Grades One and Three).* Toronto, ON: Nelson.

Meek, M. 1988. *How Texts Teach What Readers Learn.* Great Britain: The Thimble Press.

Merriam, E. 1964. *It Doesn't Always Have to Rhyme.* New York: Atheneum.

Minick, N. 1985. "L.S. Vygotsky and Soviet Activity Theory." Doctoral dissertation, Northwestern University, Evanson, IL.

Moss, R., and Stansell, J. 1983. "Wolf Stew: A Recipe for Growth and Enjoyment." *Language Arts* 60: 346–350.

Murphy, S. 1993. "Testing the Tests: The Psychometric and Theoretical Quality of Reading Tests." Unpublished manuscript.

Murphy, S. 1992. "The Basal Reader: An Update." In *Elementary Reading: Process and Practice*, edited by C. Gordon Labercane and W. McEachern, 151–166. Needham Heights, MA: Ginn Press.

Murphy, S. 1991. "Authorship and Discourse Types in Canadian Basal Reading Programs." *Reflections on Canadian Literacy* 9 (3 & 4): 133–138.

1992 Report of the National Assessment of Education Progress (NAEP) *Reading Report Card* (Executive Summary).

Nodelman, P. 1991. "The Eye and the I: Identification and First-Person Narratives in Picture Books." In *Annual of the Modern Language Association* (Division on Children's Literature), 1–30. New Haven: Yale University Press.

Ontario Ministry of Education. 1991. *Circular 14: Textbooks.* Toronto, ON: Queen's Printer for Ontario.

Pappas, C.C., Kiefer, B.Z., and Levstik, L.S. 1990. *An Integrated Language Perspective in the Elementary School: Theory into Action.* New York: Longman.

Pearson, P.D., *et al.* 1991. *On the Horizon.* Needham, MA: Silver Burdett-Ginn.

Pearson, P.D., *et al.* 1991a. *Dream Chasers: World of Reading, Volumes 1 & 2.* Needham, MA: Silver Burdett-Ginn.

Pearson, P.D., *et al.* 1991b. *A New Day: World of Reading.* Needham, MA: Silver Burdett-Ginn.

Perkins, P. 1989. "Readiness in the Basal Reader: An Update." Paper presented at the annual meeting of the Eastern Educational Research Association, Savannah, GA and at the annual meeting of the New English Educational Research Organization, Portsmouth, NH (ERIC Document Reproduction Services No. ED 306-549).

Pikulski, J.J., *et al.* 1991a. *Just Listen.* Boston, MA: Houghton Mifflin.

Pikulski, J.J., *et al.* 1991b. *Golden Threads.* Boston, MA: Houghton Mifflin.

Rennick, B., *et al.* 1984a. "At the Farm." In *One by One—Unicorn*, 40–47. Toronto, ON: McGraw-Hill.

Rennick, B., *et al.* 1984b. "In the Woods." *One by One—Unicorn*, 48–55. Toronto, ON: McGraw-Hill.

Rennick, B., *et al.* 1984c. "In the City." *One by One—Unicorn*, 32–39. Toronto, ON: McGraw-Hill.

Rennick, B., *et al.* 1984d. *Unicorn (Grades 1 and 3).* Toronto, ON: McGraw-Hill.

Rennick, B., *et al.* 1985. *Teacher's Guide and Resource Book for: One by One; Sing a Rainbow; Gingersnaps; Long, Long Ago; Star Light, Star Bright.* Toronto, ON: McGraw-Hill Ryerson.

Resnick, L.B., and Resnick, D.P. 1990. "Tests as Standards of Achievement in Schools." In *Proceedings of the 1989 ETS Invitational Conference: The Uses of Standardized Tests in American Education*, edited by J. Pfleiderer, 63–80. Princeton, NJ: Educational Testing Service.

Rhodes, L. 1981. "I Can Read! Predictable Books as Resources for Reading and Writing Instruction." *Reading Teacher* 34 (5): 511–518.

Roberts, E.E.M. 1981. *The Children's Picture Book*. Cincinnati, OH: Writer's Digest Books.

Rockwell, T. 1933. *How to Eat Fried Worms*. New York, NY: Franklin Watts.

Rosenblatt, L. 1991. "Literature—S.O.S.!" *Language Arts* 68.

Rylant, C. 1985. *The Relatives Came*. New York: Bradbury Press.

Said, E. 1993. *Culture and Imperialism*. New York, NY: Knopf.

Schon, I. 1992. "Center for the Study of Books in Spanish for Children and Adolescents." *CABE Newsletter* 14 (4): 3,4.

Schonell, F. 1972. *Hide and Seek*. Edinburgh: Oliver and Boyd.

Schwarcz, J.H., and Schwarcz, C. 1991. *The Picture Book Comes of Age*. Chicago: American Library Association.

Sergiovanni, T.J. 1992. "Moral Authority and the Regeneration of Supervision." In *Supervision in Transition: The 1992 ASCD Yearbook*, edited by C. Glickman. Alexandria, VA: Association for Supervision & Curriculum Development.

Sergiovanni, T.J. 1990. "Adding Value to Leadership Gets Extraordinary Results." *Educational Leadership* 47 (8): 23–27.

Sergiovanni, T.J. 1987. "Will We Ever Have a True Profession?" *Educational Leadership* 44 (8): 44–49.

Shannon, P. 1993. "Commentary: A Critique of False Generosity: A Response to Baumann." *Reading Research Quarterly* 28: 9–14.

Shannon, P. 1992. *Becoming Political*. Portsmouth, NH: Heinemann.

Shannon, P. 1990. *The Struggle to Continue: Progressive Reading Instruction in the United States*. Portsmouth, NH: Heinemann.

Shannon, P. 1989. *Broken Promises: Reading Instruction in Twentieth-Century America*. New York: Bergin & Garvey.

Shannon, P. 1987. "Commercial Reading Materials, a Technological Ideology, and the Deskilling of Teachers." *The Elementary School Journal* 87: 307–329.

Short, P.M., Greer, J.T., and Michael R. 1991. "Restructuring Schools Through Empowerment: Facilitating the Process." *Journal of School Leadership* 1: 127–139.

Shulevitz, U. 1985. *Writing with Pictures.* New York: Watson-Guptill Publications.

Sims, R. 1982. *Shadow and Substance.* Urbana, IL: National Council of Teachers of English.

Slapin, D. and Searle, D., eds. 1987. *Through Indian Eyes: The Native Experience in Books for Children.* Philadelphia, PA: New Society Publishers.

Squires, J. 1987. "A Reading Program for All Seasons." *Theory Into Practice* 28: 254–258.

Steig, W. 1982. *Doctor DeSoto.* New York: Farrar, Straus & Giroux.

Steptoe, J. 1987. *Mufaro's Beautiful Daughters.* New York: Lothrop, Lee & Shepard Books.

Taxel, J. 1981. "The Outsiders of the American Revolution: The Selective Tradition in Children's Fiction." *Interchange* 12 (2–3): 207–227.

Thorn, E.A., and Irwin, J.M. 1986/1987. *Expressways II.* Toronto, ON: Gage.

Tompkins, G.E., and Webeler, M. 1983. "What Will Happen Next? Using Predictable Books with Young Children." *Reading Teacher* 36 (6): 498–502.

Torbe, M. 1988. "Reading Meanings: A Discussion of the Social Definition of Literacy in Relation to School and its Approaches to Reading for Meaning." Paper presented at Post-World Reading Congress Symposium, Brisbane, Australia.

Tsuchiya, Y. 1951. *Faithful Elephants, a True Story of Animals, People and War.* Translated by T. Dykes, 1988. New York: Houghton Mifflin.

Valencia, S.W., and Pearson, P.D. 1987. "Reading Assessment: Time for a Change." *Reading Teacher* 40: 726–732.

Venezky, R.L. 1987. "A History of the American Reading Textbook." *The Elementary School Journal* 87: 247–265.

Waber, B. 1972. *Ira Sleeps Over.* Boston, MA: Houghton Mifflin.

Weaver, C. and Henke, L., eds. 1992. *Supporting Whole Language: Stories of Teacher and Institutional Change.* Portsmouth, NH: Heinemann.

Weaver, C. 1990. *Understanding Whole Language.* Portsmouth, NH: Heinemann.

Weaver, C. 1988. *Reading Process and Practice.* Portsmouth, NH: Heinemann.

Wells, G. 1985. *The Meaning Makers.* Portsmouth, NH: Heinemann.

Wilde, J. 1988. "The Written Report: Old Wine in New Bottles." In *Understanding Writing*, edited by T. Newkirk and N. Atwell, 179–190. Portsmouth, NH: Heinemann.

Willard, N. 1977. *Simple Pictures are Best*. New York: Harcourt Brace Jovanovich.

Williams, M. 1922. *The Velveteen Rabbit*. London: Doubleday.

Willinsky, J. 1990. *The New Literacy: Redefining Reading and Writing in the Schools*. New York: Routledge.

Yolen, J. 1967, 1988. *The Emperor and the Kite*. New York, NY: Philomel Books.

Zinn, H. 1980. *A People's History of the United States*. New York: Harper & Row.

BASALS REVIEWED

D.C. Heath (1989/1991/1993).
Harcourt Brace Jovanovich (1989/1993).
Holt Impressions (1984/1987/1988).
Houghton Mifflin (1989/1991/1993).
MacMillan (1990).
MacMillan/McGraw-Hill (1993).
McGraw/Hill Ryerson (1984–1985).
Nelson (1983/1986/1987/1988).
Scott, Foresman (1989/1993).
Silver Burdett & Ginn (1989/1990/1991/1992/1993).

Author Index

Subject Index